P9-DMS-730

AMELIA EARHART
FIRST WOMAN OVER THE ATLANTIC

≫TRAIL BLAZERS

Neil Armstrong

Jackie Robinson

Harriet Tubman

Jane Goodall

Albert Einstein

Beyoncé

Stephen Hawking

Simone Biles

Martin Luther King Jr.

J. K. Rowling

Amelia Earhart

Lin-Manuel Miranda

AMELIA EARHART

FIRST WOMAN OVER THE ATLANTIC

SALLY J. MORGAN

RANDOM HOUSE  NEW YORK

Text copyright © 2021 by Sally J. Morgan
Cover art copyright © 2021 by Luisa Uribe
Interior illustrations copyright © 2021 by David Shephard

All rights reserved. Published in the United States by Random House Children's Books,
a division of Penguin Random House LLC, New York.

Random House and the colophon are registered trademarks of Penguin Random House LLC.

Visit us on the Web! rhcbooks.com

Educators and librarians, for a variety of teaching tools, visit us at
RHTeachersLibrarians.com

Library of Congress Cataloging-in-Publication Data is available upon request.
ISBN 978-0-593-12458-1 (trade pbk.) — ISBN 978-0-593-12459-8 (lib. bdg.) —
ISBN 978-0-593-12460-4 (ebook)

Created by Stripes Publishing Limited, an imprint of the Little Tiger Group

Printed in the United States of America
10 9 8 7 6 5 4 3 2 1
First Edition

Random House Children's Books supports the First Amendment
and celebrates the right to read.

Contents

INTRODUCTION

FOREVER FIRST

At 9:00 a.m. on June 19, 1928, Amelia Earhart crouched between the fuel tanks in the freezing cabin of a Fokker F.VII aircraft, high above the Atlantic Ocean. She and the crew of the aircraft, *Friendship,* had taken off from Trepassey Harbor, Canada, eighteen hours earlier, with the coast of Ireland and a world record fixed in their sights. Now, surrounded by thick cloud cover, they had very little idea of where they were or in which direction they were heading. At the controls, pilot Wilmer "Bill" Stultz had been flying for hours, battling fog, snow, and driving rain. Amelia huddled in the back of the plane with little to do besides making observations in the black leather journal she'd gotten just before they left.

A BAD START

The journey had been difficult from the beginning. Turbulent weather had delayed takeoff for well over a week. Unable to take to the air, the crew members who'd been hired to fly Amelia across the ocean were spending more time drinking in the local tavern than Amelia would have liked. On the night of June 16, Amelia decided that they would take off the next day, no matter what. She may not have been the one flying the plane on this trip, but she was the reason they were all there. Plans had been made, money had been spent, and people had worked hard to ensure that she, Amelia Earhart, would be the first woman to complete the dangerous journey across the Atlantic by air.

≡ DREAMS OF FLYING ≡

From the beginning of history, people all over the world dreamed about what it would be like to fly. For hundreds of years, great thinkers and inventors drew sketches, built models, and even threw themselves off high places while attached to strange contraptions in the hope that one of their ideas would fly. With kites, hot-air balloons, and gliders, taking to the skies became possible, but it wasn't until 1903 in Kitty Hawk, North Carolina, that the dream of powered flight became a reality.

Timeline to Takeoff

c. 450 BCE   Chinese engineers
Mozi and Lu Ban invent
the first kite.

c. 405 BCE   Greek mathematician
Archytas designs a steam-powered
pigeon able to fly over 325 feet
(100 m), in Taranto, Italy. Ancient
writings suggest that the pigeon
was cylindrical in shape, with two
sets of wings, and a bladder inside that connected
to a boiler. As the bladder filled with steam from
the boiler, the increasing pressure forced the
pigeon to take flight.

1485 CE Leonardo da Vinci sketches designs for various flying machines.

1783 In Paris, France, Jean François Pilâtre de Rozier and the Marquis d'Arlandes are the first people to fly in a hot-air balloon.

1785 Jean-Pierre Blanchard and John Jeffries make the first flight across the English Channel in a hot-air balloon.

1852 Henri Giffard takes flight in the first steam-powered airship in Paris, France.

1903 Orville and Wilbur Wright make the first flight in a powered airplane in Kitty Hawk, North Carolina.

1912 Harriet Quimby becomes the first woman to fly across the English Channel.

1919 John Alcock and Arthur Brown complete the first nonstop flight across the Atlantic Ocean.

1919 British aviation company Aircraft Transport and Travel Ltd. operate the first international passenger flights between London, England, and Paris, France.

1927 Charles Lindbergh makes the first nonstop solo flight across the Atlantic Ocean.

In 1928, aviation was still very new, and people were fascinated by it. Every week, newspapers were filled with stories of the latest developments in flying technology, and with these developments came fresh feats and firsts. Recent inventions and new equipment made longer flights, including transatlantic trips, possible. Just one year earlier, famous aviator Charles Lindbergh had made history by becoming the first person to fly by himself across the Atlantic without stopping.

Famous Fliers: Charles Lindbergh

Born: February 4, 1902

Charles Lindbergh was born in Detroit, Michigan, and grew up in Little Falls, Minnesota. Charles was interested in mechanical engineering from a young age and liked to tinker with his family's car. After dropping out of college in 1922, he took flying lessons and quickly discovered that flight was his passion.

Once Charles had his pilot's license, he became an airmail pilot, flying letters and packages around the country—but his heart was set on adventure.

In 1919, a wealthy hotel owner named Raymond Orteig offered a $25,000 prize to the first person to fly nonstop from New York to Paris. Many pilots tried, and many failed—some were even killed in the attempt. Eight years later, no one had achieved the feat. Charles decided to take a chance.

But buying a plane capable of flying such a distance was expensive, and Charles didn't have the money. He asked businesspeople from St. Louis, Missouri—the town where he lived at the time—to help. They did, and in return Charles named the aircraft *Spirit of St. Louis*. On May 20, 1927, he took off alone from Long Island, New York. Landing *Spirit of St. Louis* in Paris 33½ hours later, Charles made history.

Flier fact: To earn the money needed for flying lessons, Charles worked as a wing walker and a parachutist at air shows around the country.

If Charles Lindbergh had already flown the Atlantic, what was so interesting about a woman doing it? In 1928, it was unusual for women to go on adventures. Until 1920, the government didn't allow women to vote in elections in most states in America. Most colleges did not accept women, no matter how good their grades were. Many people did not think it was right for women to have their own ambitions; they were expected to give up their careers when they got married. The public certainly did not approve of women hopping onto planes in Canada and popping up hours later on the other side of the Atlantic. But things were changing. Since women had gained the vote, they'd fought for further opportunities— including the chance to take to the skies. Female pilots like Amelia were powerful symbols of what women were capable of and just how far ambition could get them.

LADIES CAN FLY!

LET US TAKE TO THE SKIES

⋛ LAND HO! ⋛

But where was ambition leading Amelia on that cloudy morning in 1928? With fuel running out and uncertainty about their position, Bill Stultz took the plane as low as he dared in an attempt to escape the clouds. Amelia's ears screamed in pain as they went down. The crew hoped that navigator Louis "Lou" Gordon had guided them correctly and that, at any minute, they would get a glimpse of their destination, Ireland. But as the clouds cleared, the crew of *Friendship* could see only ocean. Were they completely off course? After failing to get confirmation of the direction they were heading from the ships below, they decided to keep going.

Amelia was frightened. They should have seen Ireland an hour ago, and now they weren't even sure where they were! A month before, Amelia had sat down and written letters to her parents, along with a will, in the event that the worst happened and the plane crashed at sea. Amelia had hoped the letters would never be sent. Had she made the biggest mistake of her life? Would this really be her "last grand adventure," as she had written to her beloved father?

It would not. The crew spotted a fishing boat below, then another and another, all heading on the same bearing as *Friendship*. Land must be close by! Finally, they spotted a coastline. Bill flew along it, looking for a suitable spot to land. They were dangerously low on fuel, and even though they weren't sure where they were, Bill brought the plane down in a quiet harbor. Lou hopped out onto a pontoon and tied the plane to a buoy. The crew then signaled to shore for someone to fetch them in a boat. They soon discovered they weren't in Ireland at all—they were in Wales, off the

JUNE 20, 1928

FRIENDSHIP COMPLETED
AIR VOYAGE!

REACH
HER GO
IN MIS

coast of a town known as Burry Port. That didn't matter to the crew of *Friendship*. They were safe, they had flown across the Atlantic, and Amelia would forever be the first woman to have done so.

After a night in Burry Port, Amelia left the gathering crowd and traveled to Southampton, England, to be greeted by an even bigger one. Having climbed into the plane in Canada largely unknown, she stepped out of it a household name. When she returned to New York, she was given a parade and was invited to the White House in Washington, DC, to meet President Calvin Coolidge.

JUNE 20, 1928

MISS EARHART SUCCESS

Reporters clamored for interviews. Who was this Amelia Earhart? Why had she wanted to make such a journey? What did she like to eat for breakfast? People wanted to know everything about the mysterious person who had done what no woman had done before. But what they wanted to know most of all was what she was going to do next.

CHAPTER 1

FIRST STEPS

Amelia Mary Earhart was born on July 24, 1897, in
Atchison, Kansas, in a house belonging to her maternal
grandparents. Her parents were Amy Otis Earhart and
Edwin Stanton Earhart, an ambitious young lawyer
who worked for the railroad. Amelia's grandparents
were wealthy—they had a large home that overlooked
the Missouri River and was surrounded by an orchard.
The house had many rooms, including a library, and
the family had servants to look after their every
need. Amelia's grandfather was a judge and was well
respected in the community.

Not long after Amelia was born, her mother started a baby memory book for her. In this book, Amy wrote down some of the important things that happened to Amelia when she was little—a record of all of Amelia's firsts. Amelia's first word was "Papa," and she took her first steps on August 27, 1898, when she was one year and one month old.

On December 29, 1899, Amelia got a late Christmas present: a little sister named Grace Muriel Earhart, who would go by Muriel. Amelia now had someone to share both her adventures and her baby book with. To celebrate her little girls, Amy included a quotation about the works of the famous English playwright William Shakespeare.

"Shakespeare has no heroes, but only heroines."
—John Ruskin

Amy hoped her daughters would live heroic lives, which is not something that can be said of all mothers of girls born at the turn of the century. In 1900, society expected little girls like Amelia and Muriel to grow up to be wives who supported their husbands and raised children to become ambitious young men and obedient little girls. Thankfully for Amelia, her mother didn't share this view. Amelia's parents believed that girls should be given the same education and opportunities that boys had.

Women in 1900

The world Amelia and Muriel were born into was very different from the one we know today, especially for women and girls. Women at the turn of the century did not have suffrage, which meant they were not permitted to vote in elections in most states, including Kansas. Many people believed women should rely on the men in their lives to vote in their best interests.

At this time, most colleges refused to admit women. But that wasn't because women weren't smart enough. Many people thought that a woman's education should prepare her to keep a home and raise children and that subjects such as engineering and literature would distract her from her primary purpose.

Most women and girls did not take part in sports, either. It was thought that exercise could stop women from being able to have children, and so women were discouraged from participating in such activities.

Women's fashion at this time was also very different from what women wear today.

In 1900, women's clothes weren't very practical or comfortable. Restrictive garments such as corsets gave women tiny waists but made many physical activities—even breathing!—difficult.

While women were allowed to work, their employers did not expect, and often did not permit, white, middle-class women to continue working after they were married.

⋛ FREE-THINKING FASHIONS ⋛

Whereas most white, middle-class girls like Amelia and
Muriel had to wear stiff dresses with petticoats unsuited
to running, jumping, and climbing trees, Amy dressed her
daughters in poofy short trousers known as bloomers,
which she sewed herself. Wearing these, the girls could run
fast, jump high, and get themselves into all sorts of trouble.

Loose-fitting
fabric for
comfort.

Lace
and flounces
tear easily.

Tight
around the
waist.

Hard-wearing
material for
doing handstands.

Dark color
doesn't show dirt.

Poofy
skirt not
good for
cartwheels.

No flounces to
rip or tear.

Delicate
fabric is
harder to clean.

"We felt terribly 'free and athletic'; we also
felt somewhat as outcasts among the little
girls who fluttered along in their skirts."

Amelia Bloomer

Bloomers were named after another Amelia. Amelia Jenks Bloomer was born in 1818 and grew up to become a women's rights campaigner, a newspaper owner and editor, and an influential fashion reformer. Corsets were hazardous to women's health, and Bloomer thought women should wear clothes that made it easy for them to move. Bloomer urged women to try new styles and was one of the first women to wear loose-fitting pants not as an undergarment, as they were originally intended, but as trousers.

Amelia nicknamed her sister "Pidge," and because Muriel couldn't quite pronounce her sister's name, Amelia went by "Meelie." As well as playing with each other, the sisters enjoyed spending time with their cousins, Lucy and Katherine Challis—nicknamed "Toot" and "Katch"—who lived nearby. Together they played a game they called Bogie, in which they drew fantastical maps of an imagined faraway world they named Cherryville. The maps showed all the monsters and dangers they would encounter on the way. With the maps in hand, Meelie, Pidge, Toot, and Katch

climbed into a broken carriage in their grandparents'
barn and journeyed as far as their imaginations could
carry them, without ever leaving the barn. These games
could last several hours and, according to Amelia, were
some of the most frightening and exciting adventures
she would ever have.

I can never be as terrified by
anything met within the real world
as by the shadowy play creatures
which lurked in the dark corners
of the hay mow to attack us.

⋲ A ROLLER-COASTER RIDE ⋲

In addition to make-believe journeys, Amelia liked to
go on real ones, too. When she was seven years old,
her father, Edwin, took her and the family to one of
the biggest fairs the world had ever seen—the St. Louis
World's Fair in Missouri. Here, Amelia saw exhibits
from all over the globe and tried foods she had never
tasted before. She also rode on her first roller coaster.
She loved the speed and the thrill of the ride so much
that she was determined to build her own in her
grandparents' backyard. With the help of her uncle
and some friends, she nailed together planks of wood
and arranged them to form sloped tracks. For the car,
they used a wheeled crate, big enough for a child to sit
in; and to make sure that the car would slide down the
rails, they greased the wooden tracks with lard.

Amelia went first. Muriel looked on as Amelia set
the cart at the top of their homemade track and
pushed herself off. It was quite the ride. Amelia rattled
and bumped down the track so fast that the cart
bounced off the rails, launching her into the sky before
she landed in a heap. Amelia bruised her lip and tore
her clothes in the accident, but it was worth it.

The St. Louis World's Fair

From April 30 to December 1, 1904, about 20 million people traveled to St. Louis, Missouri, to visit the Louisiana Purchase Exposition, which became known as the St. Louis World's Fair. Representatives from 43 states and over 60 countries exhibited at the fair in enormous "palaces." Exhibitors showed off their state's or country's culture as well as their latest inventions and innovations, in the hope of attracting trade. In this time before television or internet, the fair let visitors see wonders from across the globe, such as a Japanese garden and a reconstructed Egyptian street.

Among the new technologies on display was the first X-ray machine, a wireless telephone, and, in the Palace of Transportation, some of the world's first cars. If visitors tired of all the new technology, for entertainment there was a circus and a zoo with exotic animals. There were also roller coasters and an observation wheel that towered 265 feet (80.8 m) above the fairground. When visitors got hungry, they could sample exciting cuisines from all over the world, including waffle cones and cotton candy, which are said to have been invented at the fair.

⋛ EARLY ADVENTURES ⋛

Amelia's family owned a large black dog they named
James Ferocious. Lovable and friendly to the family,
James Ferocious was quite different when approached
by people he didn't know! One day, some boys from
the neighborhood were passing the house when James
began to bark fiercely. The boys, thinking the dog was
tied up securely, began to tease him. James barked
even louder, tugging at his tether until he pulled free!
Terrified, the boys climbed onto the roof of the shed,
shouting for help as James barked frantically below.

On hearing the boys' cries and James Ferocious's yelps, Amelia ran outside to see what was happening. Even though she was just six years old, Amelia wasn't afraid. When she saw what was going on, she calmly but firmly called her angry dog away from the boys. She led James Ferocious into the house, allowing the relieved boys to escape to safety. When Amelia's mother learned what had happened, she asked what Amelia had been thinking, approaching James Ferocious when he was behaving so aggressively— she could have been attacked! Amelia said she hadn't had time to think about being afraid.

⋛ FLYING HEADFIRST ⋜

Amelia was always on the hunt for adventure and loved going sledding in the winter. Unlike most of her girlfriends, who sat upright in the sled, Amelia careered down slopes headfirst on her stomach, the snow flying in her face!

One snowy day when she was about six, Amelia dived onto her sled, slapping it onto the snow with her stomach to get it whizzing down a hill. She held tight as the sled moved faster and faster toward a road at the bottom. Amelia planned to skid straight across the road, but as she got closer, she saw a horse and carriage approaching. She was heading right for them, and she was going too fast to stop! Thinking quickly, she steered her sled toward the horse, skillfully guiding it between the animal's legs.

Had Amelia been sitting upright, she would have crashed hard into the poor animal's side. Thanks to Amelia's headfirst sledding and quick thinking, neither she nor the horse got hurt.

Amelia also loved to play with her friends from elementary school. They had mud-ball fights and picnics. The girls also played among the bluffs along the

banks of the fast-flowing Missouri River. Amelia and
her friends liked to explore the caves that tunneled
deep into the soft stone, daring one another to see
who had the courage to travel the farthest into the
darkness. Amelia and her friends used the caves as
their special hideouts. To make sure others didn't
venture inside, they put up signs at each entrance
warning "trespassers." As the young adventurers
weren't quite sure how to spell *beware*, they made
two different signs.

BEWEAR!

BEWARE!

⋛ LOST IN THE LIBRARY ⋛

Amelia might not have been able to spell *beware*, but she did very well at school and worked hard in her lessons. The Earhart girls played outdoors whenever they could, but when they did have to stay inside, Amelia liked to read in her grandfather's library. She had to lie on the floor because some of the books were so large and heavy that they were difficult to read any other way, but Amelia didn't care.

Two of Amelia's favorites were *Black Beauty* and *The Tale of Peter Rabbit,* but she also enjoyed books by authors such as Charles Dickens and Alexandre Dumas. These books were filled with adventures in faraway places— adventures like the ones she hoped to have someday.

NEW JOURNEYS

Soon, the Earhart sisters would swap their imaginary adventures for real ones. Edwin's job working for railroad companies meant he had to travel a lot. Sometimes his family traveled with him, though often he traveled with Amy or alone, leaving the girls in the care of their grandparents.

In 1907, Edwin secured a job with a rail company in Des Moines, Iowa. Amy traveled with Edwin to Des Moines, and together they looked for a house suitable for the whole family. Edwin and Amy sent for their daughters to join them in 1908.

CHAPTER 2

ON THE MOVE

Amelia's life in Des Moines was very different from the life she had enjoyed in Atchison. In Kansas, Amelia had had the run of a large house, but in Iowa, the family's home was smaller, and there were no servants to pick up after them. In Atchison, the girls had attended an exclusive private school, but in Des Moines, they were supposed to go to a local public school, where Amelia's mother was advised to cut the girls' hair to stop them from getting lice. Because of her sheltered upbringing, this made Amy nervous, so she sent for one of the girls' former schoolteachers to teach them at home instead. After less than a year, the teacher decided to return to Kansas. Amy felt she had no choice but to send Amelia and Muriel to the public school.

Despite all of this, it was a happy time for the Earharts. Edwin worked hard and got promoted to head of his department. His salary doubled, and the family was able to live more comfortably. Each summer, the Earharts traveled to Worthington, Minnesota, where they went sailing and fishing on Lake Okabena. As well as playing on the lake, Amelia learned to ride on an old pony named Prince. The girls liked to feed Prince "pies," which they made from sugar cookies topped with clover.

⋛ FAIRGROUND FLYING ⋚

With more money to go around, Edwin and Amy were able to take the girls on other fun outings, too. On one of these trips in 1908, when Amelia was eleven years old, her father took Muriel and her to the Iowa State Fair. There were merry-go-rounds, sideshows, and pony rides, as well as sweet treats such as ice cream and cotton candy. The girls bought fashionable hats, known as peach basket hats, made of paper, which they were very pleased with.

At the same Iowa State Fair, Amelia got her first glimpse at what would become the focus of her life. Edwin loved airplanes and was excited to see one fly. Once the girls had had their fill of rides and ice cream, Edwin took them to a field on the outskirts of the fairground to watch as a small plane took to the sky. Amelia wasn't very impressed.

It was a thing of rusty wire and wood and looked not at all interesting.

⋝ AIR SHOWS ⋜

In 1908, the airplane was a new invention. It had been just five years since two brothers took the first-ever flight in a powered airplane at Kitty Hawk, North Carolina. The flights made by the Wright brothers lasted only seconds, but technology was moving fast. Air shows like the one at the Iowa State Fair were all the rage. People looked on in wonder as daring pilots, known as barnstormers, donned goggles, climbed into the cockpits, and accelerated along a flat piece of land until they launched into the air.

These pilots were daring not because of any tricks they performed (those came later) but because early airplanes were made of wood, wire, and fabric—nothing like the sleek, sturdy planes that soar through the skies today. Accidents were common, giving these shows an element of danger that made them even more exciting to those who dared to watch.

Famous Fliers: The Wright Brothers

Wilbur Wright
Born: April 16, 1867

Orville Wright
Born: August 19, 1871

Orville and Wilbur Wright grew up in Dayton, Ohio, and from a young age loved to learn about how things worked. One day their father bought them a toy helicopter powered by a rubber band. The boys were fascinated by it.

Orville and Wilbur began experimenting with their own flying machines in 1896. But the brothers realized it wasn't windy enough in Dayton for their experiments, so they wrote

to the National Weather Service for a list
of suitable places. They chose a spot in
Kitty Hawk, North Carolina.

On December 14, 1903, on a windswept beach,
Wilbur lay on his stomach behind the controls
of the *Wright Flyer*. He steered down the
beach to take off, but as the *Flyer* was about
to lift off the ground, it pitched forward
and crashed. Wilbur was unhurt, but the *Flyer*
needed repairs.

Three days later, Orville took a turn behind
the controls, and this time the engine did
not stall. Orville flew for the very first
time while Wilbur looked on. Orville's flight
lasted just 12 seconds, but it was 12 seconds
that would change the world forever.

Flier fact: Neither Wilbur nor Orville went
to college or graduated from high school.

WILBUR WRIGHT   ORVILLE WRIGHT

⋚ LIFE OFF THE RAILS ⋚

Life for the Earharts wasn't all lake vacations and air shows, though. Amelia's father, Edwin, struggled with alcoholism. In 1910, Edwin's drinking caused him to lose his job, and the family was forced to leave town so that he could find employment elsewhere. The Earharts moved around a lot during this time, from Des Moines to Kansas City and eventually to St. Paul, Minnesota, in 1913. Each time they settled, Amy and the girls hoped that this would be a fresh start. But it never was. Edwin lost job after job, and the family had a hard time making ends meet. In addition to money problems, Amy and the girls found it hard to cope with Edwin's bad temper.

With each move came a new school for Amelia and Muriel. Amelia attended a total of six different high schools before she graduated. Starting a new school was never easy, but the girls threw themselves into their studies as much as they could, and both were excellent students.

In St. Paul, Amelia went to Central High School, where she attended dances and played on her high school basketball team. Her favorite subjects were

Latin and algebra. Though her grades were good, Amelia got annoyed when her male classmates' achievements seemed to be celebrated more than hers. Like any teenager, she also argued with her parents about how late she should be allowed to stay up at night, but she didn't sneak out or break the rules.

Eventually, Edwin lost his job in St. Paul, too. He thought he had found another one in Springfield, Missouri, but after taking the family all the way there, he discovered it had been a mistake. The man he was supposed to replace wasn't retiring after all. There was no job. This was the last straw for Amelia's mother, who felt she had no choice but to separate from her husband. She moved in with friends in Chicago, taking Muriel and Amelia with her.

This was a very sad time for Amelia. Her life had transformed from being a part of a happy family, respected in society, to one broken apart by her father's drinking. Instead of being welcomed wherever they went, as they had been when Amelia was little, the Earharts were now gossiped about and pitied.

⋛ AMELIA TAKES CHARGE ⋛

The move to Chicago came at an important time in Amelia's life: her senior year in high school. Amelia had dreams of becoming a doctor, and to have the best chance, she wanted to make sure she was at the best school. She didn't like the school Muriel was going to attend—she didn't think the science laboratories were good enough. After touring a number of other high schools in the area and interviewing their principals, Amelia settled on Hyde Park High School.

Hyde Park High School was ahead of its time in many ways. It had sports teams for both boys and girls, and lots of after-school clubs, including a choral society and a newspaper. But Amelia struggled to fit in and didn't take part in these activities.

In Atchison and St. Paul, Amelia's life had been filled with friends, but in Chicago, Amelia was lonely. She missed her friends and her father, whom she loved very much. At the end of each day, Amelia left school as soon as the bell rang, preferring to study by herself. She kept her eyes on her future, working hard at chemistry and physics. She also flourished in English, reading four times the number of books assigned for her course.

$\gtrless$ SCRAPS OF THE FUTURE $\lessgtr$

As a teenager, Amelia kept scrapbooks of articles she clipped from magazines about women who inspired her. They were lawmakers, farmers, and film directors— women living independent lives filled with adventure, lives like the one she hoped to have when she graduated.

Amelia kept scrapbooks throughout her life, eventually filling more than 20 of them with press clippings of her own achievements and adventures.

Amelia's hard work paid off, and in 1915, she graduated. Amelia was pleased to graduate, but she was not close to her classmates, so she chose to skip her graduation ceremony. She didn't even bother to pick up her diploma. Proof that Amelia's classmates never got to know her can be seen in the caption printed next to her yearbook picture, which describes her as "meek."

"Meek loveliness is around thee spread."

Amelia was tired of being moved around by others; she was ready to make a move of her own.

⋝ HAPPY DAYS ⋜

Following her graduation, Amelia took a year off from education to visit some of her old friends and family. Meanwhile, her father had stopped drinking, and her mother had moved back to Kansas to be with him. Amelia and Muriel joined their parents, happy to have their family back together again. Around this time, Amy came into some money from her mother's estate. Her mother had died some years earlier, but Amy's inheritance was put into a trust, as her mother believed that Edwin couldn't be relied upon not to spend it. Amy went to court to get this overturned, and the family was able to live in style once more.

Amy wanted to use some of the money to pay for her daughters' education. She enrolled Amelia in the Ogontz School, a finishing school near Philadelphia. In 1916, finishing schools like the Ogontz School offered subjects such as domestic engineering, which included housekeeping and childcare, as well as subjects geared toward young women who wanted to attend college, including chemistry, astronomy, history, and Latin. Amy hoped it would be the perfect place to prepare Amelia for studying medicine. Muriel wanted to become a teacher, and she chose to study at St. Margaret's, a college preparatory school in Toronto, Canada.

Amelia, Muriel, and their mother stayed in touch while the girls were away at school, writing letters to each other frequently. It is clear from Amelia's letters that she was much happier at the Ogontz School than she had been in Chicago. Amelia wrote about her busy schedule and the things she and her friends got up to outside of their studies. Amelia had made good friends at the school, with girls she felt were similar to her. She took part in after-school activities, going on walks and playing for the school hockey team.

Sometimes Amelia found herself having a bit too much fun with her new friends, though. On one occasion, the school called her mother for a stern talk after Amelia was found climbing onto the roof of one of the buildings wearing just her nightgown.

Despite her antics, Amelia was popular with the staff and students. Her grades were excellent, and she was elected to the position of vice president of her class during her second year, as well as secretary of the local chapter of the Red Cross. To help prepare her for medical school, Amelia studied first aid. As she learned how to care for injured patients, Amelia became increasingly aware of the war being fought in Europe.

The Great War

World War I started in Europe in 1914. Tensions had been rising for some time, due to nations competing for land and resources. To defend themselves, some countries formed groups promising to protect one another, should they be attacked. Great Britain, France, and Russia formed a group called the Allies. Germany made a similar alliance with Austria-Hungary and Bulgaria to form the Central Powers.

On June 28, 1914, Archduke Franz Ferdinand of Austria was assassinated by a Serbian terrorist. In response, Austria-Hungary declared war on Serbia. Soon many of the countries in Europe and their territories overseas, including Canada and countries in Asia and Africa, were at war. Many hoped the fighting would end quickly. However, new weapons technology meant that it became the bloodiest war the world had ever seen.

In April 1917, the United States entered the war, joining the Allies. The US government sent thousands of troops to Western Europe to fight.

By the time World War I ended in November 1918, it had claimed the lives of over 10 million soldiers from around the world and injured millions more.

CHRISTMAS IN CANADA

In December 1917, Amelia went to visit Muriel in
Toronto. There, Amelia saw the real effects of the war.
The United States had only been at war for six months,
and at Ogontz, it had seemed almost exciting, with men in
sharp uniforms marching to brass bands. But in Toronto,
the situation was quite different. As a member of the
British Commonwealth, Canada had been at war for
three years, sending troops to help Great Britain and the
Allies. Injured men, returning from Europe's battlefields,
arrived at the military hospital in Toronto in droves.
Amelia was shocked to see so many young men on
crutches—but she knew these were some of the luckier
ones. The military hospital was filled with others who
were blinded, paralyzed, and burned beyond recognition.
Many of these soldiers were younger than she was.

Amelia wanted to do something to help. She decided to speak to her mother about leaving school to volunteer in the hospitals. After what she had seen in Toronto, giving up her studies didn't seem like such a big deal.

As senior class president, Amelia had helped write the class motto:

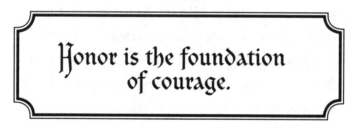

Honor is the foundation
of courage.

Amelia believed in this motto and thought the most honorable and courageous thing she could do was to help the wounded soldiers in any way possible, even if it meant not graduating.

CHAPTER 3

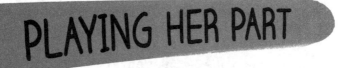

PLAYING HER PART

To contribute to the war effort, Amelia enrolled in a first-aid class and trained to be a nurse's assistant.

Amelia was not alone in wanting to do whatever she could. Women all over the United States, Canada, and Europe were playing their part in the war effort by going to work for the first time. As the war went on, more and more men were sent to the battlefields in Europe, leaving their day jobs vacant. The government campaigned for women across the country to do their duty by filling these posts.

They're doing their part

Time to roll your sleeves up!

World War Women

During World War I, the number of women entering the workforce increased dramatically. Business owners put aside many of the rules that had previously prevented women from joining the workforce. Women went to work in factories that manufactured weapons, airplanes, and chemicals that would be needed to win the war. They also became farmers, ticket collectors, and bank employees. For the first time in history, women were allowed to join the military, taking on the office jobs vacated by men who had been sent to Europe. Some women even traveled overseas to help in army hospitals near the battlefields.

⋛ LIFE ON THE WARD ⋚

Once she had completed her training—which included learning how to scrub down a hospital ward correctly to avoid infection, and how to help dress a wound—Amelia worked as a volunteer at the Spadina Military Hospital in Toronto. At Spadina, Amelia spent her time caring for the wounded soldiers. Amelia was on duty from 7:00 a.m. to 7:00 p.m. She kept the ward clean, assisted the nurses on their rounds, handed out ice cream, and even helped boost morale by playing tennis with some of the recovering patients.

Because Amelia had studied chemistry, she was also allowed to work in the dispensary, where pharmacists prepared medicines. She helped measure out the medications given to the patients. During the 1918 flu outbreak, Amelia worked night duty on an overcrowded ward, doling out medicine to the sick.

The 1918 Influenza

In 1918, a deadly influenza known as the
Spanish flu spread quickly around the world.
To stop the flu from spreading, many US
cities closed schools and banned libraries
from lending books. New York City staggered
businesses' opening times to prevent
overcrowding in the streets and subway. People
were advised to avoid shaking hands and to
stay indoors when possible. Despite these
measures, the virus continued to spread.

It is estimated that from 1918 to 1920,
over 500 million people were infected with
Spanish flu, and 20 to 50 million people
died worldwide, including 675,000 Americans.
Unlike other outbreaks of flu, when infants
or elderly people were most affected, the
1918 flu sickened otherwise strong and
healthy people. More US soldiers were killed
by the flu virus than were killed in action
during the war.

Symptoms of the Spanish flu included fever,
headache, nausea, and diarrhea. Many patients
developed pneumonia, a dangerous lung infection.

⋝ HIGHS AND LOWS ⋜

Although dangerous and often sad, working in the
hospital did have some perks. Many of Spadina's
patients had served as airmen, and Amelia enjoyed
listening to their stories of flying. When they had
recovered enough, some of these airmen took Amelia
and her sister to the local airfield to watch the trainee
pilots take off and land.

"I was thrilled by the sting of the snow on my
face as it was blown back from the propellers
when the training planes took off on skis."

Amelia worked up to fourteen hours a day treating
the soldiers suffering from the flu, until she, too,
became infected with the virus. Amelia became so sick
that she was hospitalized and had to stay in bed for
more than two months. When she finally recovered,
Amelia returned to the ward but worked so hard that
she became run down and got sick again, this time with
a painful sinus infection.

Amelia was in Toronto, recovering from her infection, at the end of World War I. When the war was declared over on November 11, 1918, Amelia took to the streets with her friends. Things got pretty wild as young men ran around, knocking off people's hats and pelting the crowd with bags of flour.

⋛ GOOD MEDICINE ⋚

Soon Amelia's sinuses became so painful that she had to have surgery. To recover, Amelia went to stay with her sister and mother in Massachusetts. Muriel had moved there to continue her education at Smith College. At this time, Amelia's father was on a business trip in California.

Even though Amelia was unwell, she did not like being idle. To keep busy, she volunteered for a charity, learned to play the banjo, and took an automobile-repair class.

With the war over and her sinuses on the mend, Amelia's thoughts returned to her education. She had not enjoyed being a patient, but her hospital stay and her work as a nurse's assistant had renewed her interest in becoming a doctor. She enrolled in a premed course at Columbia University in New York.

Amelia took courses in biology, chemistry, and French literature. Even though she was now grown up, Amelia still loved to go on adventures, just as she had as a child. Together with friend and fellow student Louise de Schweinitz, Amelia explored every inch of campus. One of their favorite things to do was to climb up the dome of the university library and go out on the roof.

> I was probably the most frequent visitor on top of the library dome.

Although she was having a good time and even breaking a few rules, Amelia studied hard. Yet she soon grew to realize that she didn't want to become a doctor anymore. She thought she might like to go into research, but the idea of treating patients no longer appealed to her. In May 1920, Amelia was ready to leave New York, but where would she go?

MOVING WEST

Not long after Amelia enrolled at Columbia, her father's business trip to California became a permanent move. Edwin set up a legal practice in Los Angeles, and Amy moved to be with him. They rented a large house on West Fourth Street, where they hoped Amelia and Muriel would join them. Amelia, unsure of what her next steps should be, did just that. Her parents were thrilled to have her back. They hoped that Amelia would continue her education in California or get married and start a family nearby.

Edwin and Amy's hopes were raised even further when Amelia stared dating a chemical engineer named Sam Chapman, who was renting a room in her parents' house. Sam was tall and handsome, and the pair had a lot in common—they both liked reading and discussing politics.

Sam introduced Amelia to a political organization known as the Industrial Workers of the World (IWW). Sam believed that people had the right to fair pay from their employers and should receive help from the government when they were unable to find work.

In addition to discussing politics and attending meetings, Amelia and Sam enjoyed playing tennis, swimming, and going to the theater together.

⋛ SHARED INTERESTS ⋜

Amelia was pleased to be reunited with her father in California. Since she had watched the airmen in Toronto, Amelia shared her father's interest in aviation. Amelia and Edwin went to air shows almost every weekend. She loved to watch the planes as the pilots raced and performed tricks, such as daring nosedives and upside-down flight.

On Christmas Day in 1920, Amelia and Edwin went to the Winter Air Tournament at a new airfield in Long Beach, California. During one of the many aerobatic displays, an aircraft dived dramatically toward the crowd. Many of the spectators were frightened, but Amelia was confident in the skill of the pilot and sure that, at the last second, he would pull out of the dive and climb back into the clouds. Amelia was right, and she was exhilarated.

Amelia wanted to feel what it was like to perform a trick like that. She begged her father to find out if she could take a ride in an airplane. Edwin knew better than to stand in the way of any scheme his determined daughter devised. He agreed to find out more and arranged for Amelia to take a flight with a pilot named Frank Hawks.

Famous Fliers: Frank Monroe Hawks

Born: March 28, 1897

Frank Monroe Hawks was born in Marshalltown, Iowa. Frank trained as a pilot in Long Beach, California, and joined the army during World War I, serving as a flying instructor, training new recruits.

After the war, he was also one of the world's first pilots of commercial passenger flights. He was a test pilot for aircraft manufacturers, and he set many intercity and transcontinental speed records during his career.

Flier fact: Frank was the first person to fly a glider from California to New York.

⋛ TAKING FLIGHT ⋚

Three days after the show, Amelia and her father met Frank at Rogers Field, a small dirt airfield in an LA suburb. Amelia took her seat at the front of the plane, with Frank sitting behind. After a short trip down the uneven runway, the plane lifted into the air. They were flying!

Their flight lasted only ten minutes, but that was enough for Amelia to decide that she wanted to become a pilot.

By the time Frank brought the plane down, Amelia knew she would go up again as soon as she could.

"As soon as we left the ground, I knew I myself had to fly."

That evening, Amelia raised the subject with her parents. Edwin thought it was a good idea. Amelia was delighted by her father's reaction and began looking into how to become a pilot. After asking everyone she knew who had an association with flying, Amelia found an instructor who was willing to teach her. She had everything in place and was excited to start—she just needed her parents to pay for the lessons.

But when Edwin found out how expensive it was, he changed his mind. Lessons could cost as much as a dollar per minute, which was a lot of money in the 1920s. An aspiring pilot had to spend thousands of minutes in the air, mastering the skills needed to qualify for a license. Now that Edwin was working again and Amy had come into her inheritance from her mother, the Earharts were not poor, but they were not so well off that there was enough money for Amelia to get her pilot's license on a whim. Amelia was discouraged, but she didn't give up.

Amelia decided that if her father wouldn't give her the money to learn to fly, she would have to earn it herself. She took a job as a stenographer at a telephone company, where she typed up notes with a special shorthand typewriter. She also helped in her father's office and worked as a photographer at a local photography studio. Amelia even took work driving a gravel truck. She was determined to find a way to make her dream come true.

Amelia's father could see how hard she was working and that she

was determined to learn to fly. He was proud of her and told her he would help her pay for lessons if she could find a suitable instructor. Amelia knew of just the person—a woman named Neta Snook.

Famous Fliers:
Mary Anita "Neta" Snook

Born: February 14, 1896

As a young girl, Neta loved all things mechanical, and by the time she was in college, she had set her heart on learning to fly. The first flying school she applied to rejected her, as it did not admit women, but Neta persevered and found a school that would teach her.

Although she was unable to fly during the war due to a government ban on all nonmilitary flying, Neta worked for the British Air Ministry, overseeing the production of planes that were to be sent to Europe. After the war, Neta bought a broken-down plane—a Canadian Canuck—and rebuilt it. When it was ready, she completed her training. For a while Neta flew people around in Iowa, but she was frustrated by the winters, when it was too cold to fly. So she moved to California, where she could fly all year round, and began barnstorming.

In February 1921, not long after Amelia began lessons, Neta became the first woman to enter a men's air race. She placed fifth!

Flier fact: Neta gave up flying in August 1922 to marry William Southern. She didn't fly again until she was 81 years old.

Amelia and her father went to meet Neta at Kinner Field, an airfield in Los Angeles, to ask if she would agree to give Amelia lessons. Neta had wild, curly red hair and was little more than five feet tall, and in a letter to her sister, Amelia wrote that Neta "dresses and talks like a man." At their first meeting, Neta wore a flying jacket and men's breeches. Amelia, on the other hand, had her hair braided neatly and was wearing a stylish brown suit with a long skirt.

I hope Amelia isn't going to start dressing like that!

Neta took an instant liking to Amelia and was impressed by her elegant clothes, even though they weren't suitable for flying. Neta thought Amelia looked like she would make a good student and that it would be fun to teach another woman. She agreed to instruct Amelia in her own plane, and the two became good friends.

CHAPTER 4

BECOMING AN AVIATRIX

On January 3, 1921, after finishing work, Amelia rode the streetcar to the end of the line and walked three miles to get to Kinner Field for her first lesson with Neta. Amelia hadn't bought her own flying clothes yet, so she wore riding breeches and a brown riding jacket. She was ready to take to the sky, but she would have to wait. Her first lesson was spent learning to taxi Neta's plane around the bumpy airfield. In fact, because of bad weather, Amelia managed to log only four hours in the air in her first two months.

When Amelia did get to fly, she found that Neta had some interesting teaching methods. Neta carried a rubber hammer, and if student pilots became frozen with fear while flying, she would bop them on the head with it!

Amelia loved being at the airfield and went there whenever she wasn't working one of her many jobs. As Amelia learned to fly, she realized she needed to wear clothes suited to trudging through dusty fields and climbing in and out of planes. Not many women wore pants at this time, and although Amy had sewn Amelia bloomers for her daring adventures as a child, she didn't think young ladies should wear trousers. Nevertheless, Amelia, like Neta, wore men's breeches, which were more comfortable and practical for flying.

One day, on her way to the airfield, she was picked up by a motorist who was driving with a little girl in the back seat. The child said Amelia didn't look like an "aviatrix"— a female pilot—because all the female fliers she had seen in magazines had short hair. Short hair was more practical for flying, because it fit neatly beneath the leather flying helmets pilots often wore. It was becoming more fashionable, too. But Amelia had a plan. She was cutting her hair shorter gradually, an inch at a time, so as not to attract her mother's attention. Amy thought young ladies should wear their hair long, so to hide her trimmed tresses, Amelia wore her hair pinned up at home.

⊰ FLYING SOLO ⊱

Eventually, the time came for Amelia's first solo flight. She got the plane up and down safely, despite a bit of a bumpy landing. Amelia wrote later that she managed to do everything wrong during the flight, but she was pleased to have finally done it. She knew she had a lot to learn if she wanted to get her license, but she was on the right track.

To mark her first solo flight, Amelia bought herself a new leather flying jacket. She hoped it would help her look like a real pilot, but there was one thing wrong with it—it was new. All of the pilots Amelia knew owned jackets that were scuffed and stained with oil. Amelia's friends at the airfield made fun of her shiny new jacket. Amelia, determined to look the part, made her jacket dirty on purpose.

There's still something missing.

⋛ TRICKS OF THE TRADE ⋚

Amelia had to learn how to navigate and control the aircraft in difficult situations. To do this, she decided to study many of the tricks that had wowed her at the air shows.

Side slip: To descend in a sideways direction. The wings of the plane are tipped, and the plane moves sideways more quickly than it moves forward. Useful when coming in to land.

Stall: To fly directly upward so that the plane loses forward power. The plane begins to fall from the sky.

Tailspin: To descend spinning nose-first due to loss of airspeed.

Zoom: To ascend very quickly at a steeper angle than can be maintained in normal flight.

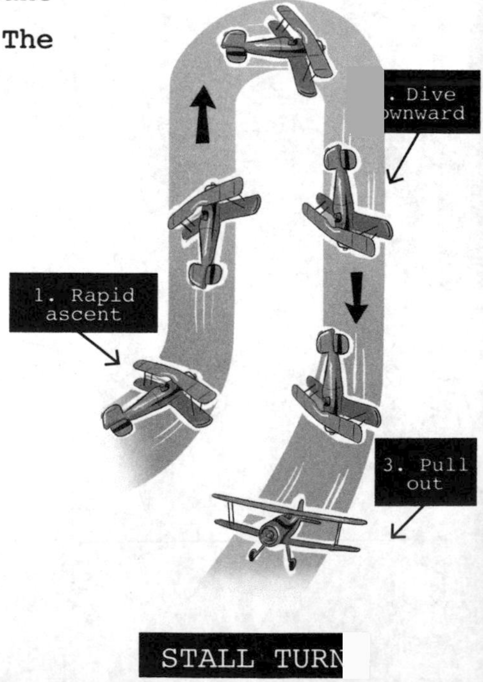

2. Dive downward

1. Rapid ascent

3. Pull out

STALL TURN

Dive: To descend very quickly at a steep angle with or without the engine running.

Bank: To turn the plane in a circle with the wings at an angle.

⋛ A PLANE OF HER OWN ⋚

Amelia was learning to fly in Neta's Canuck, but soon she wanted her own plane. Amy was impressed by how hard her daughter was working and agreed to help pay for it. Amelia knew which plane she wanted: a bright yellow Kinner Airster. Amelia's friends at the airfield weren't sure if it was a good fit for a beginner—the small plane could be hard to control—but Amelia's heart was set. She bought the plane and named it *The Canary*.

It was in *The Canary* that Amelia finished her initial training. She took the test to become a pilot on December 15, 1921, and was granted her license. It had been less than a year since Amelia watched Frank Hawks wow the crowd at an air show, and now she was able to perform in them herself. A young woman pilot was still a rare phenomenon, and many people came to see her fly. Among them were her mother and father, and Sam, whom she saw whenever she wasn't at the airfield or working to earn money for lessons.

Great Planes: Kinner Airster
The Canary

Seats:	2
Wingspan:	21 ft. (6.4 m)
Manufacturer:	Kinner Airplane and Motor Corporation
Engine:	Single L5 radial piston
Horsepower:	60 hp
Speed:	85 mph (137 kmh)
Max height:	14,000 ft. (4,267 m)
Weight:	606 lb. (275 kg)
Manufacture date:	1921

Unfortunately for Amelia, when Neta got married in 1922, she decided to leave her flying days behind her. Amelia needed to find someone else to help hone her skills.

⋜ RECORD BREAKING ⋜

Amelia's new teacher was John "Monte" Montijo, an engineer who worked at the airfield. Monte had been a pilot in World War I. He was fantastic at aerobatics and became one of the first stunt pilots to appear in movies. With Monte, Amelia learned complicated tricks, and her confidence in the air grew. She wanted her own place in the record books.

On October 22, 1922, Amelia invited her father and sister to watch her perform in a small air show called a "fly-in" at Rogers Field. Amelia took off, as she had done many times before, but she had no intention of performing her usual tricks. This time, Amelia wanted to take her plane higher than any woman had gone before. Edwin and Muriel were shocked to see Amelia's little plane disappear into the clouds. Flying high was dangerous—pilots were known to pass out from lack of oxygen when flying at high altitudes, and instruments within the aircraft could freeze due to low temperatures.

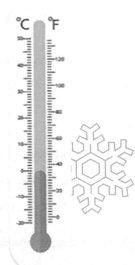

The Canary had to fly upward through thick, freezing fog. Amelia climbed higher and higher until she reached 14,000 feet (4,267 m), the highest that a woman had ever flown. Amelia brought her plane down quickly and made a rushed landing. The crowd was amazed when they heard what she had done. Instruments carried on board *The Canary* verified the height of the flight. Amelia's altitude record was broken within just a few weeks, but she had proven to herself, and to her watching family, that she could be a record-breaking flier.

⋛ MOVING EAST ⋚

In 1924, Amelia's family lost a lot of money when the trucking and mining businesses they had invested their savings in failed. The stress of these money troubles was too much for Amy and Edwin's relationship. They decided to get a divorce. Amelia's sister was studying at Radcliffe College in Boston, Massachusetts, and Amelia and her mother wanted to travel from California to join her. But during this difficult time, Amelia's sinus problems returned. She couldn't fly, because the dramatic changes in air pressure she experienced when ascending and descending aggravated her sinuses. A doctor told her that she would need expensive surgery. In need of money and unable to fly, Amelia sold her plane and bought a little yellow car instead. She called it the *Yellow Peril* and used it to drive her mother across the country to Boston.

The journey took them six weeks, but Amelia and Amy turned what could have been a long, boring drive into a fun road trip, stopping at many of the national parks along the way. They caused a stir riding in the *Yellow Peril*—two women alone on the road was almost as scandalous as women flying!

⋛ BACK TO SCHOOL ⋚

In Boston, Amelia was admitted to Massachusetts
General Hospital for treatment for the sinus problems
that she had struggled with since 1918. The treatment
was a success, and Amelia reported feeling better than
she had in years. She decided to return to her studies,
first at Columbia in the fall of 1924, and then in the
summer of 1925 enrolling at Radcliffe with her sister.
To help pay her tuition, Amelia taught English lessons
to foreign students and found she liked it very much.
Amelia loved to learn but still couldn't settle on what
she wanted to do, so she left without completing her
degree.

Sam followed Amelia to Boston, where he asked
her to marry him. Amelia accepted the proposal but
didn't think she wanted to get married anytime soon,
and she wasn't sure if she ever would. She knew that
even though Sam loved her and supported her flying,
like most young men at the time, he would assume that
Amelia would not have a career of her own. Amelia
was twenty-eight years old. She had seen many of her
friends get married and she'd watched as they gave up
their ambitions and settled down with husbands and

children. Amelia knew she didn't want that, but what *did* she want? Sam and Amelia eventually parted ways, but they remained good friends.

In 1926, Amelia applied for a job at Denison House, a school for immigrant children, and was offered the position. There, Amelia met children from all over the world who had come to America with their families in the hope of finding a better life. Amelia taught various subjects, but first she had to teach many of her students to speak English.

Amelia's work at Denison House didn't leave much time for flying, but she squeezed in what she could. She got to know some of the local fliers by joining, and becoming vice president of, the Boston chapter of the National Aeronautic Association. She used some of her wages from Denison House to pay for more hours in the air, and even judged a model aircraft competition.

⋛ AN EXCITING CALL ⋜

One afternoon in April 1928, Amelia was in her classroom when a student knocked on her door to tell her she had a phone call. Amelia didn't recognize the name of the caller, and as she was busy with the children, she asked that the person call back later. But the student who brought the message insisted that the caller had said it was important. Reluctantly, Amelia left the classroom to take the call.

The person at the other end of the line was former World War I US Army Captain Hilton H. Railey. He was calling to ask Amelia if she would like to become the first woman to make a transatlantic crossing in an airplane. Charles Lindbergh had become the first man to fly solo across the Atlantic the year before, in the *Spirit of St. Louis*. Unlike Charles, Amelia would be a passenger, not the pilot. Railey explained that a woman named Amy Guest had purchased the plane and organized everything for the trip but had had to pull out at the last minute because her family would not let her go. Amy had asked Captain Railey to find a replacement. Having heard about Amelia's work with the National Aeronautic Association, he hoped she would be up for the challenge. The trip was being overseen by George Putnam, who had published a book by Charles Lindbergh after his flight, catapulting him to fame. Captain Railey was a friend of George's and believed it would be a wonderful opportunity for Amelia.

A BIG OPPORTUNITY

Amelia was unsure about the offer—she loved flying, but she was happy at Denison House and knew the trip across the Atlantic would be dangerous. Before Lindbergh's successful thirty-three-and-a-half-hour flight, six men had died attempting to fly across the Atlantic in pursuit of the $25,000 Orteig Prize, and nobody had succeeded at a solo attempt since.

Amelia weighed everything in her head. Her pros-and-cons list may have looked something like this:

PROS
- I would become the first woman to cross the Atlantic by air.
- I would get to be called "captain."
- It could be the start of something amazing.

CONS
- I wouldn't actually get to do any flying.
- I wouldn't get paid, unlike the rest of the crew.
  The pilot, Wilmer Stultz, is to be paid $20,000!
- Transatlantic flight is very dangerous. PEOPLE HAVE DIED!

After discussing the offer with George, Amelia believed it was too big a chance to miss. She knew that although she wouldn't get paid for the trip, the media attention could lead to all kinds of adventures. Amelia decided that she would do it—she would become the first woman to make a transatlantic flight.

George now had everything he needed for the event to go ahead. He had a crew and a plane called *Friendship*, and now he had the female pilot he'd been looking for. But they weren't the only ones hoping to claim the title of first woman to fly across the Atlantic.

If they were going to attempt the flight, they had to do it soon. Other women, who had their own planes and crews, were making plans to do the same thing.

Famous Fliers: The Contenders
Mabel Boll

Born: December 1, 1893

Mabel Boll was a wealthy socialite who was willing to pay $50,000 to become the first woman to be flown across the Atlantic. She had made one attempt to fly from England in 1927, but bad weather had stopped her crew from taking off.

Flier fact: The glamorous Mabel Boll was said to have had a sweater made of gold.

Famous Fliers: The Contenders
Thea Rasche

Born: August 12, 1899

German stunt pilot Thea Rasche, otherwise known as the "Flying Fraulein," was also planning to attempt a flight across the Atlantic.

Thea had had problems with her plane and with her financial backers but assured the press her plans were well underway.

Flier fact: Before becoming a pilot, Thea went to agricultural college and became a farm inspector.

ꓤ ON THEIR WAY ꓥ

When Amelia had first heard about the attempt, she asked Railey if she would be able to fly the plane, or at least take the controls for part of the flight. Railey told her it would be unlikely. *Friendship* was unlike any plane Amelia had flown. It had two more engines than she was used to and was equipped with complex instruments Amelia had never used before.

Great Planes:
Friendship

Seats:	8—12 (most stripped out to accommodate fuel tanks)
Wingspan:	71 ft. (21.6 m)
Manufacturer:	Fokker
Engine:	Three air-cooled Wright Aeronautical Corporation Model J-5C Whirlwind nine-cylinder radial engines
Horsepower:	220 hp
Speed:	118 mph (190 kmh)
Max height:	14,000 ft. (4,267 m)
Weight:	6,724 lb. (3,050 kg) without pilot or fuel
Date of manufacture:	1927

Friendship had another difference, too. Instead of wheels for taxiing around on a runway, the orange-and-gold plane was fitted with pontoons—hollow cylinders made of metal that could float on water. The pontoons allowed *Friendship* to take off and land on water, which might come in handy if the crew needed to make an emergency landing halfway across the Atlantic. To fly the plane, George hired a man named Wilmer "Bill" Stultz. Bill had a lot of experience flying at sea, having served as a pilot for the US Navy. Bill and Amelia were joined by Lou Gordon, an airplane mechanic who had trained in the army. Bill and Lou got the plane ready at an airfield in Boston, while Amelia kept her distance. George didn't want her to be seen with the plane in case news of their attempt leaked to the press.

Amelia boarded *Friendship* in Boston on June 3, 1928, to fly to Trepassey, Canada, on the tip of Newfoundland. Starting from Trepassey would make the Atlantic crossing as short a distance as possible. The crew hoped to fly straight there from Boston and take off for Ireland soon after, but things didn't go according to plan. Soon after takeoff,

Friendship's cargo door flew open. Amelia had to hold it shut until Lou tied it with a strap. The crew had checked with the National Weather Service before they left, but as they flew toward Trepassey, they were engulfed in thick fog. Bill decided to land in Halifax Harbor and wait for the fog to lift. They spent the night in a hotel nearby.

Friendship took off again after breakfast the next day and landed in Trepassey five hours later. Back in Boston, George had told the press about *Friendship* and Amelia, and the news had spread. There were journalists everywhere the crew looked, all wanting to get the scoop on *Friendship* and its journey.

Unfortunately for Amelia and the crew, weather updates sent by ships on the Atlantic warned of strong winds and stormy conditions that would make flying very dangerous. They would have to wait.

Amelia hoped the storms would clear quickly so they could make their attempt, but she was worried about more than just the weather. Bill passed the time in the local tavern, drinking heavily. Amelia was concerned that even if the weather did improve, Bill might have drunk too much alcohol to fly the plane safely. Amelia was getting impatient. She hadn't left her job in Boston to sit around doing nothing on the coast of Canada. She told Bill to get his act together—they were going to fly the next day, no matter what.

CHAPTER 5

THE FLIGHT TO FAME

The following morning, on June 17, 1928, the weather cleared and *Friendship* was ready. At 11:00 a.m. Amelia found herself clutching a stopwatch in the cabin of *Friendship* as it gathered speed across the bay.

If they could reach a speed of at least fifty miles per hour (eighty kmh), *Friendship* could take off, and they would finally be on their way. *Friendship* shuddered and shook as it swept across the water on its pontoons. Amelia held her breath as the plane reached twenty, thirty, forty … fifty miles per hour, and then, at sixty, *Friendship* took to the sky.

It was going to be a long flight, and to compensate Amelia for not being the pilot, George made her captain of the crew, but she still didn't have much to do. George had given her a journal in which to record any interesting observations for a book he intended to publish when she returned. She described the flight as "a voyage into the clouds," because although Amelia noted seeing the North Star appear above the wing tip, and the dawn at 3:15 a.m., for much of the flight, she was able to observe very little.

It was like heading into fantastic gobs of mashed potato.

The cloud cover was a problem for Bill, too. Unable to see how high they were flying or what direction they were headed in, he had to rely almost entirely on the instruments on board to navigate.

When they had only a few hours of fuel left, Bill took the plane below the clouds to check their flight path. If they were on course for Ireland, they would see ships beneath them heading east and west as they sailed between America and Ireland. Bill hoped they'd be able to follow the ships sailing east to a port where they could land. But when they emerged, they were surprised to see an ocean liner sailing from north to south! Ships usually sail east or west in the Atlantic, so the crew members of *Friendship* worried that they were flying in the wrong direction. They feared they were lost. The crew tried to radio the ship, but there was no response. Bill circled the ship—a signal to the crew to paint the bearings, or the direction they were headed in, on the deck—but there was still no response.

Thinking quickly, Amelia wrote their request on a

piece of paper and put it in a bag with a couple of oranges. Bill flew over the ship while Amelia leaned out of the hatch to drop the bag onto its deck. She missed. The message and the oranges plopped into the water.

With little more than an hour's worth of fuel remaining, the crew discussed what they should do. If they accepted that they were lost, their best bet was to land near the ship below and be hauled aboard. But if they did that, all of their record-breaking efforts would have been for nothing. They felt helpless. They made the decision to press on in the hope that land was close.

⋛ WELCOME TO WALES ⋚

Half an hour later, the crew saw small fishing boats, which, according to *Friendship*'s instruments, were heading east. Because small fishing boats usually stay close to shore, land had to be nearby. Lou was the first to spot cliffs on the horizon. But was it Ireland? At this point, the crew didn't care. *Friendship* landed on the water just outside Burry Port in South Wales, twenty hours and forty minutes after taking off. The crew waited to be spotted by someone and for a boat to be sent out to them, but no one came.

Amelia could see three men working on the railroad close to the shore, but if they were curious about the plane tied to a buoy not half a mile from them, they didn't show it. Bill climbed onto one of *Friendship*'s pontoons and shouted, but still no one came.

Amelia waved a towel out the window, and someone waved back but then returned to his work. It was not the welcome they had hoped for, but because they were in Wales, no one had been expecting them.

Eventually, police officer Norman Fisher approached them in a boat. He took Bill ashore to telephone friends waiting for news. Amelia and Lou waited in *Friendship*—it was important that they stayed until the press had arrived, to make sure there were some photographers to capture her record-breaking feat. They needed some people to celebrate with, too.

Though it was slow to start, news of the travelers spread. Crowds gathered, and once Amelia made it to the shore, she was nearly crushed by well-wishers eager to see the now-famous woman. Amelia said she felt like she shook hands with ten thousand enthusiastic Welsh people. That night in her room at the hotel in Burry Port, Amelia was too excited to sleep, even though she had been awake for more than thirty hours. After seeing the enthusiasm of the crowd there, she knew that the reception back home would be even bigger. Her life would never be the same again—all Amelia needed to do now was decide what she wanted to do with it.

⋛ MORNING STAR ⋚

By the time Amelia woke up, after six hours' sleep, she was one of the most famous women on the planet. But she had nothing to wear—her flying clothes were salty and dirty from the trip, and in order to keep the aircraft as light as possible, she hadn't packed a change of clothing. Amelia had to borrow from a woman who lived in the village.

Once Amelia was dressed and had eaten breakfast, she was ready to leave, but first she had to get through the crowds. Captain Railey, who had sailed to Southampton, England, ahead of the flight, helped her. As there was no way of knowing exactly where *Friendship* would land, he had waited in Southampton with a seaplane on standby, ready to fly to wherever *Friendship* set down.

Railey guided Amelia as she answered questions, posed for pictures, and shook hands until she thought her arm might fall off. When Amelia was done, she climbed aboard *Friendship* again. The crew was ready to fly, but this time Amelia would be at the controls. Railey had arranged a large reception in Southampton, with members of the British and American press. They wanted a picture of Amelia flying and climbing out of *Friendship* with the crew.

From Southampton, Amelia and the crew traveled to London, where they were treated like celebrities. Amelia was invited to dine with British politicians, including Winston Churchill and the first female member of Parliament, Lady Nancy Astor, who asked about her journey as well as her work at Denison House.

Amelia had expected publicity, but nothing like this. Some reporters called her "Lady Lindy" after record breaker Charles Lindbergh. Amelia wasn't happy about this. Charles Lindbergh had flown the plane, and she hadn't!

I was just baggage, like a sack of potatoes.

≋ AMELIA MEANS BUSINESS ≋

On June 28, Amelia, Bill, and Lou sailed back to New York City on a ship called the SS *President Roosevelt*. When Amelia arrived, she rode in an open-topped car through the crowds that had lined the streets to greet her. Ticker tape rained down from above. At city hall she was awarded the key to the city by the mayor of New York.

Amelia was invited to similar events in thirty-two
cities across the country, but she agreed to just
three—New York, Boston, and Chicago. Thankfully,
George Putnam, who had advised Lindbergh after his
transatlantic trip, knew how to help Amelia make the

most of the limelight. He soon became her manager. If people wanted to interview Amelia or hear her speak, they had to pay. If they wanted her to endorse their products, such as cars or clothes, they would have to pay. If they wanted to read how she felt about the transatlantic trip, they could buy the book she was about to finish writing, which George would publish, just as he had done with Lindbergh.

George coached Amelia on what to wear, how to pose for pictures, and even how to smile. In the months that followed, George arranged for Amelia to give over one hundred speeches and countless interviews. Amelia became an editor for *Cosmopolitan*, a popular lifestyle magazine, writing articles about travel and women's courage. She used her platform to speak out on women's rights and to spotlight the achievements of other female fliers.

Amelia could see the power and independence her fame gave her. She was able to help her family, who had often struggled for money. She brought attention to issues she cared about and was offered opportunities she'd never dreamed of. But once her book was finished, Amelia wanted to get away from all the attention, and she knew just how to do it.

In England after her transatlantic flight, Amelia had bought a small Avro Avian airplane from Lady Mary Heath, a famous aviatrix. Lady Mary had used the plane in 1928 to make a record-breaking solo flight, becoming the first person to fly from Cape Town, South Africa, to Croydon, England. The journey of more than ten thousand miles took Lady Mary three and a half months and included stops in Uganda, Egypt, and Sudan.

Lady Mary Heath

Lady Mary Heath was a record-breaking pilot, an Olympic athlete, a writer, and a women's rights activist. In the 1920s, Lady Mary fought the International Commission for Air Navigation for women to be allowed to become commercial pilots—pilots who transport people or goods on planes. Lady Mary won and became Great Britain's first female commercial pilot.

Amelia shipped the Avro Avian to New York. It arrived with a note that read:

To Amelia Earhart from Mary Heath, Always think with your stick forward.

When up in the air, pilots need to maintain their plane's speed to keep it flying. To do this, pilots fly with the stick (or controls) in a forward position. To Amelia, the message meant that it was time to take to the sky again!

Great Planes: Avro Avian

Seats: 2

Wingspan: 28 ft. (8.5 m)

Manufacturer: Avro, Great Britain

Engine: Cirrus II air-cooled inline engine

Horsepower: 84 hp

Speed: 102 mph (164 kmh)

Max height: 18,000 ft. (5,500 m)

Weight: 1,130 lb. (513 kg)

Date of manufacture: 1927

⅀ COAST TO COAST ⅀

Amelia flew across the country, hopping from city to city in her new plane. She pinned maps to her clothes to help her navigate when she was in the air, but when these were torn away by the wind, she had to fly low to read the road signs she saw along the way. Most of the time, Amelia landed in fields to refuel, but when she got lost over New Mexico, she caused a stir by bringing her plane down on a main street. Amelia thought of her trip as a vacation, but her flight from coast to coast and back turned out to be yet another first—the first time a woman had flown from the Atlantic to the Pacific Coast and back again.

Refreshed from her trip, Amelia returned to New York ready to get back to work. She became a spokesperson for some of the first commercial airlines that would carry people wherever they needed to go. Amelia's role was to use the fame and influence she had gained from her transatlantic flight to encourage travelers to choose flying over other forms of travel, such as driving or taking the train.

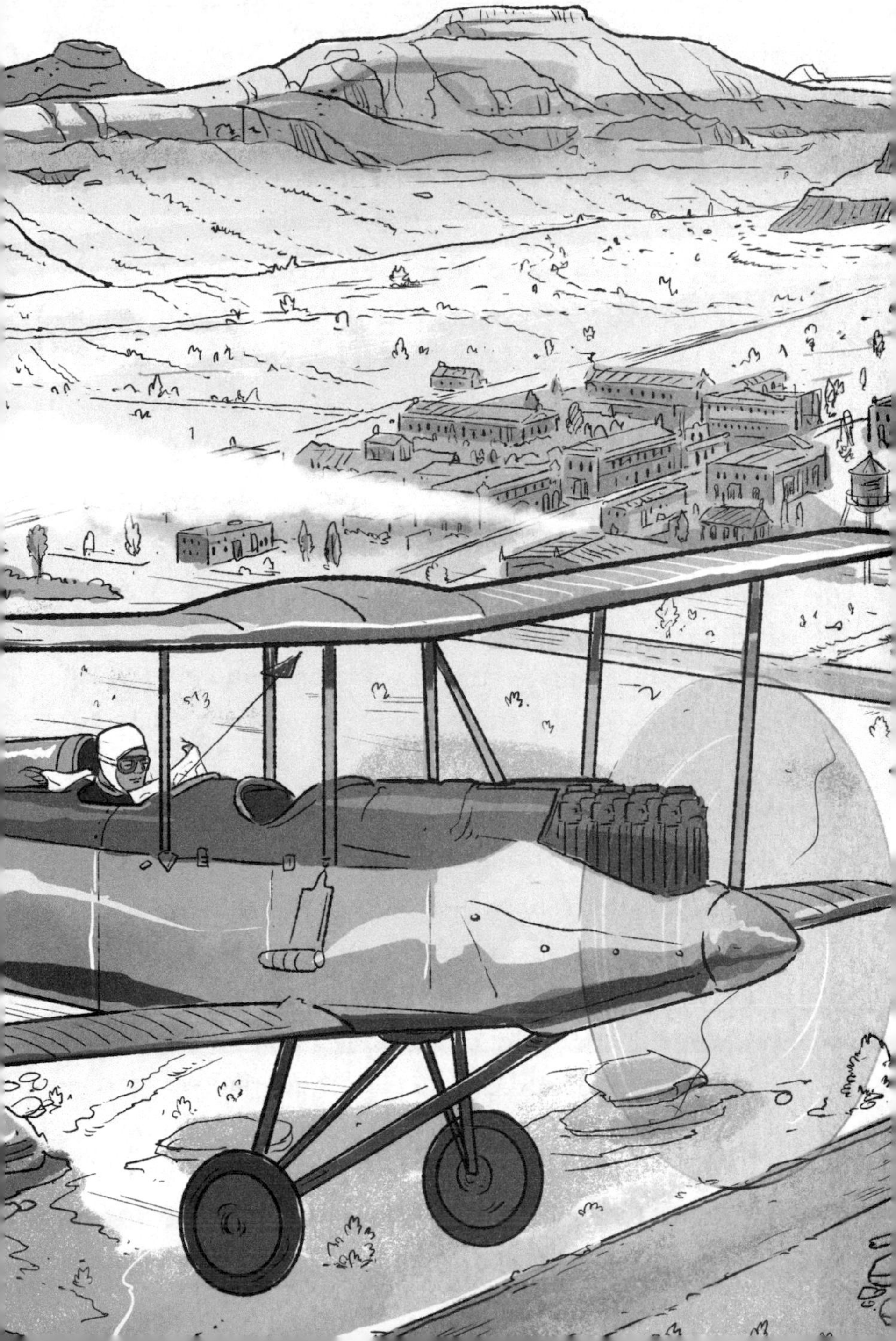

Fear of Flying

Today, flying is considered one of the safest ways to travel, but in the 1930s, people needed a bit of persuading to get on a plane. In the early days of flying, there were lots of accidents, and this, along with airsickness and rough weather that sometimes caused flights to be diverted, made many people hesitate to climb aboard. But things were improving. At first, airplanes were used to deliver mail, not people, but it wasn't long before companies realized the opportunity. Travel by air was quicker than any other mode of transport and had the potential to be much more convenient than trains or cars.

In the United States, four major commercial airline companies—American, TWA, United, and Eastern—did everything they could to attract wealthy passengers, including decorating their cabins in the latest styles and offering tasty meals. The airlines advertised in newspapers and magazines and hired celebrities to talk about why people should choose them the next time they needed to take a trip.

≡ DARING DEEDS ≡

Amelia's fame and reputation for daring deeds opened up
not just business opportunities, but also the chance for new
adventures. In 1929, Amelia was invited to Block Island,
Rhode Island, to ride aboard a submarine. Having already
flown high above the surface of the Atlantic Ocean,
Amelia's adventurous spirit couldn't resist exploring what
lay beneath. During the trip, Amelia became one of the
first women in the world to exit a submerged submarine,
and she even got the chance to walk on the bottom of the
ocean wearing a diving suit. Amelia's dive lasted about
fifteen minutes, but she didn't get the chance to see much
more than an old milk bottle and a clamshell.

⋚ A NEW PLANE ⋚

With the income from her appearances, lecture tours, and book sales, Amelia had enough money to buy herself another plane. In 1929, she bought a Lockheed Vega 5B, the biggest plane she had piloted yet.

Great Planes: Lockheed Vega 5B
Little Red Bus

Seats:	1 pilot; 6 passengers (unmodified)
Wingspan:	41 ft. (12.5 m)
Manufacturer:	Lockheed Aircraft Company
Engine:	Air-cooled, supercharged, nine-cylinder radial engine
Horsepower:	420 hp
Speed:	185 mph (298 kmh)
Max height:	19,000 ft. (5,791 m)
Weight:	2,564 lb. (1,163 kg) without pilot or fuel
Date of manufacture:	1927

⊑ THE 1929 WOMEN'S ⊏ AIR DERBY

The 1929 Women's Air Derby was the first women-only airplane race in the United States. With the adventures of female aviators such as Amelia Earhart and Lady Mary Heath filling the papers, more and more women had learned to fly. The derby was a chance for these women to show what they were capable of and prove that they were able to fly aircraft as skillfully as male pilots could. Many members of the press, however, did not take the women seriously. They nicknamed the race the "Powder Puff Derby" and referred to the entrants as "Ladybirds" and "Sweethearts of the Air" in their articles. But the women who took part were experienced fliers with many hours in the air.

The route wasn't easy. The journey was split into nine stages from Santa Monica, California, to Cleveland, Ohio, crossing over the Rocky Mountains. Organizers became nervous that the course was too dangerous for women and wanted each pilot to be accompanied by a male navigator. Amelia and the other female pilots who had entered the race were insulted. They refused to fly unless they could fly alone. Faced with having no contestants at all, the organizers dropped the idea of male navigators.

The derby didn't go without a hitch. Of the nineteen planes that started the race, only eleven finished the course. Some pilots flew off course, some crash-landed during refueling stops, and one woman, Marvel Crosson, died after her parachute failed to open when she bailed out over the mountains. Amelia herself had a lucky escape after her plane flipped over when she came in to land on a refueling stop, damaging the propeller. Thanks to her many years of experience with planes, Amelia was able to make the repairs and get into the sky again quickly enough to finish in third place, behind Louise Thaden in first and Gladys O'Donnell in second.

Despite the dangers, the female pilots had shown the world just how brave and talented women could be. In the process, many had become good friends. A few days after the race, Amelia invited the fliers to a meeting in her hotel room and suggested they set up a club for female pilots.

The Ninety-Nines

To begin, the flying club called themselves the Twenty-Sixes, after the number of women who first joined. But as more and more female pilots became members, they settled on the name the Ninety-Nines.

The Ninety-Nines helped members get jobs in flying and also kept records of their achievements. Amelia was their first president. She had worried that her fame would cause her to lose the respect of other female fliers, but they loved her as much as everyone else did. Amelia used her position in the Ninety-Nines to encourage other women to learn how to fly.

Today, the Ninety-Nines is an international organization with thousands of members around the world. The club promotes the advancement of women in flying through education, scholarships, and mutual support.

As well as encouraging others to take to the skies, Amelia set her sights on more record-breaking flights. In 1930, she broke the speed record three times, reaching a maximum speed of 180 miles per hour (290 kmh).

"Records as such may or may not be important, but at least the more of them women make, the more forcefully it is demonstrated that they can and do fly."

⋛ SAYING GOODBYE ⋜

In September 1930, Amelia received a telegram from her father's new wife, Helen. She wrote that Edwin was dying and that he had asked to see Amelia. Edwin had been unwell for some time, his health damaged by alcohol.

Amelia flew to visit him in Los Angeles. She stayed as long as she could but eventually had to return to work in New York. Edwin died shortly after she left.

Amelia was heartbroken by his death, but she didn't have much time to grieve. She needed to work. Amelia's sister, Muriel, was now married and lived in Boston with her husband, Albert Morrissey, and their new baby. They all relied on Amelia for money. The family was struggling financially, along with millions of Americans at the time.

The Great Depression

The 1920s had been wonderful for the United States. Business was booming, and people had money to spare. They would use this money to invest in the stock market by buying shares in businesses, which raised the value of the shares. Many people became rich buying and selling shares. Everyone, from bankers to street sweepers, invested their money in the stock market, some even borrowing money from banks to be able to do so.

But in 1929, the economy began to slow down. People became nervous and sold their shares, often for far less than they had paid. By October, there was panic. More and more people sold their shares for record-low prices. On October 29, 1929, a day that became known as Black Tuesday, $30 billion was wiped from the stock market in a single day. Many people lost their life savings, and others were left in debt, unable to pay back the money they had borrowed. Businesses closed, and by 1930, four million Americans were out of work. That number rose to 15 million by 1933. Without work, people couldn't earn the money they needed to feed their families. This period was known as the Great Depression.

⋛ NEW PROMISES ⋚

Amelia looked for advice and support from her manager and friend, George Putnam. George had been by her side since her transatlantic flight, and they fell in love. George proposed to Amelia in October 1930, and she accepted. Amelia had been set against marriage for so long, but she hoped George would allow her to live the life she wanted. To make sure, Amelia wrote George a letter asking him to promise her the freedom to be herself.

Please let us not interfere with the other's work or play, nor let the world see our private joys or disagreements. In this connection I may have to keep some place where I can go to be myself, now and then, for I cannot guarantee to endure at all the confinement of even an attractive cage. I must exact a cruel promise and that is that you will let me go in a year if we find no happiness together.

George agreed to her conditions. On February 7, 1931, in a quiet ceremony at George's mother's house in Noank, Connecticut, they married. Because of Amelia's fame, she and George kept their plans a secret, not even inviting her family.

⋛ A NEW OLD CHALLENGE ⋚

In January 1932, Amelia was ready for a new challenge. She wanted to fly the Atlantic again, but this time she wanted to do it alone. She asked George if he would mind, and he promised to help her in any way he could.

It had been nearly five years since Charles Lindbergh had made his solo flight across the Atlantic, and no one had managed it since, man or woman. To make sure she was able to back out of the flight if she wanted to, Amelia and George hid her plans from the press. To do this, Amelia hired out her plane to a fellow explorer named Bernt Balchen. Balchen's job was to fit the plane with all the latest navigational tools Amelia needed for her flight, but he pretended that he was readying it for an Antarctic trip of his own.

Once the plane was ready, Amelia learned how to instrument-fly—using the new technology on board to help her navigate through bad weather and clouds, which would make it hard to see out of the cockpit windows.

The date Amelia and George chose for her to take off was important: May 20, 1932, was exactly five years after Charles Lindbergh had taken off for his solo flight. Amelia revealed her plans to a group of reporters on May 18, shortly before flying to Harbour Grace, Canada, to begin her attempt. Many believed that such a flight would be impossible for even the most skilled female aviator and that it shouldn't be attempted. Amelia didn't agree.

I wanted to prove it to myself, and to anyone else interested, that a woman with adequate experience could do it.

CHAPTER 6

BREAKING NEW RECORDS

On the evening of May 20, 1932, Amelia climbed into the cockpit of her Lockheed Vega in Harbour Grace. She had a copy of that day's newspaper and a packed lunch of hot chocolate, a chicken sandwich, and a can of tomato juice.

Amelia knew her journey would not be easy. She had made the trip before, after all. Alone, she would have to make all the decisions that Bill Stultz and Lou Gordon had made together. She had learned about Atlantic weather patterns and practiced instrument flying, but had she done enough? Amelia told reporters that she was confident she would make it, but she was nervous when she took off at 7:12 p.m.

The journey started well. The weather was good, and Amelia flew into a glorious sunset. But then things started to go wrong. When flying at what she believed to be around 12,000 feet (3,658 m), Amelia looked at her altimeter and found the hands on the dial spinning wildly. It had stopped working. For the rest of the flight, she would have no way of knowing how high she was flying.

As night fell, so did the clouds, and soon storms above the Atlantic were jolting the Vega up and down. Amelia flew above the clouds to avoid much of the storm, but flying so high made the moisture on her wings freeze. The ice made the wings heavy and the Vega hard to control, and ice in her airspeed indicator meant she couldn't tell how fast she was flying. Amelia flew lower, in warmer air, to try to melt the ice. She flew as low as she dared, just above the ocean, until a sudden fog made flying so low without an altimeter too dangerous. Amelia had to climb higher, and for the rest of the flight she struggled to find a safe height where her wings didn't freeze and her instruments worked the way she needed them to.

Amelia battled through the night, despite discovering a leak in one of her fuel tanks. Fuel dripped down her neck, and the fumes gave her a headache. It had been an uncomfortable trip, and after thirteen hours of flying, Amelia longed for it to be over. She was relieved when she saw the coast of Ireland, but she knew she wasn't safe yet. Amelia would need to find a suitable place to land. She followed a railroad in the hope it would lead to a city with an airfield, but instead she saw farmland. Amelia flew on until she spied a suitably flat pasture and brought the Lockheed Vega down, before taxiing toward a cottage.

The first person she spoke to was Dan McCallion, a cowherd who rushed toward the plane after Amelia landed.

She'd done it! It had been a difficult night, but she'd flown across the Atlantic in fourteen hours and fifty-six minutes—more than twice as fast as Lindbergh had flown it.

The owner of the farm, Mr. Gallagher, drove her into town so that she could call George. In America, George had suffered a difficult night, too. The Press Association had called to inform him that a plane believed to be Amelia's had crashed near Paris. But a couple of hours after news of the crash broke, George got a call from Amelia saying that she was safe. She had become the first woman to fly solo across the Atlantic, and the only person to have completed the journey more than once.

Amelia accepted an invitation to stay the night close to where she'd landed, so she could recover from her long flight.

⋛ READ ALL ABOUT IT ⋚

By morning, news had spread. Six thousand people crowded into the Gallaghers' field! Amelia's plane was too damaged for her to fly it on to London, so she arranged for it to be taken apart and shipped there separately. On May 22, Amelia flew to London in a plane provided by a news corporation that had paid for exclusive interviews about Amelia's flight.

Congratulations rolled in. Amelia had done an amazing thing, not just for herself but for women everywhere.

MAY 23, 1932

SHE MADE IT!

"You have demonstrated not only your own dauntless courage but also the capacity of women to match the skill of men in carrying through the most difficult feats of high adventure."
—President Herbert Hoover

This time, Amelia accepted the honors graciously, knowing that she had achieved them for her skill as a pilot. She had been behind the controls on this flight, and she was only the second person in the world who could claim to have flown across the Atlantic alone.

In London, Amelia was invited to teas and dinners in her honor, and even got to dance with the Prince of Wales. Amelia's damaged plane was put on display in Selfridges, a luxury department store. Amelia then traveled to meet George in France, where she was awarded the Knight's Cross of the Legion of Honor from the French government. Together, they toured Europe for almost a month, traveling to Italy to meet the pope, and then to Belgium, where they were introduced to the king and queen. On June 15, Amelia and George set sail on a ship called the SS *Île de France*. As the ship left the harbor bound for New York, a small fleet of French airplanes flew overhead, dropping flowers onto the deck for Amelia.

Back in New York, she was treated to another parade. Her transatlantic flight had established her as one of the greats. Before the solo trip, even though she had many flying hours, Amelia had worried that some people saw her as more of a celebrity than a real pilot. Nobody could say that now.

BACK TO WORK

Amelia was more famous than ever, and she was determined to use her fame for good. Not long after she returned to the United States, she was back at work, writing a book about her experience flying solo across the Atlantic. She joined the National Woman's Party and wrote letters to editors of newspapers on the subject of women's rights to work and earn a living.

People weren't just interested in Amelia's opinions on flying or women's rights; they also wanted to know what she liked to wear! As one of the most photographed women in the world, the newspapers often commented on her clothes. Seeing an opportunity, George proposed a deal with Macy's, suggesting that Amelia design a line of clothes for its department stores.

Amelia took this job very seriously. Between speaking engagements and public appearances, she worked with a seamstress to design many items. Amelia believed clothes should be practical and allow women to move freely, like the bloomers her mother had made for her and Muriel when they were children. To keep with the theme of aviation, Amelia suggested making the blouses out of parachute silk and designed the buttons and clasps to look like nuts and bolts and little silver propellers.

≥ FLYING THE FIRST LADY ≤

In March 1933, Amelia was invited back to the White House to attend the presidential inauguration of Franklin Delano Roosevelt. Amelia arranged for his wife, Eleanor, and some female reporters to join her on a hop over Washington, DC. The First Lady enjoyed the flight so much that she said she would like to learn to fly herself.

⋛ RECKLESS RECORDS ⋚

Amelia wanted to perform even more daring feats, but the routes she was flying were getting harder and more dangerous. Some people accused her of being reckless in pursuit of publicity.

Nevertheless, in 1934, Amelia decided she wanted to fly solo across the Pacific Ocean from Honolulu, Hawaii, to Oakland, California. This journey, like her transatlantic flights, would be long and dangerous. It had been flown before, but no one had done it alone. Amelia was determined to become the first. When word got out about Amelia's new record attempt, the press criticized the flight as being too risky—ten pilots had died trying to fly a similar route solo. Many journalists also questioned who would pay for a search-and-rescue mission, should Amelia crash somewhere in the Pacific. Despite the negativity, Amelia was committed to doing it. She had the Vega fitted with new equipment, including a two-way radio, and was sure both she and her aircraft could handle the trip.

In Honolulu, on January 11, 1935, Amelia sailed into the air without a hitch. As she neared California, she announced over the radio, "Am on course, will be in any moment now." She landed at the Oakland Airfield, where thousands of fans were waiting to greet her. Even President Roosevelt sent his congratulations!

"You have shown even the 'doubting Thomases' that aviation is a science which cannot be limited to men only."
—President Franklin Roosevelt

Amelia had proved yet again that she could do it, but she didn't rest long. She'd set her sights on another challenge, again following in the footsteps of Charles Lindbergh.

⋛ ONE LAST HOP ⋚

On April 19, 1935, three months after her Pacific flight, Amelia flew from Los Angeles to Mexico and then on to New York. She was the first woman to fly the route solo, and she shaved fourteen hours off the time set by Charles Lindbergh.

When she landed, she was greeted by over fifteen thousand people. Members of the crowd hoisted Amelia onto their shoulders and carried her to the hangar.

But after years of touring the world and smashing records, Amelia was getting tired. Some people believed George was pushing her too hard in order to make money, but if there was pressure, it wasn't just coming from George. Amelia's family still relied heavily on her for money, and there was also pressure from the press—everyone wanted to know what the famous record breaker was going to do next.

For a change of pace, Amelia decided to take a job at Purdue University as a career counselor for women. The president of the university said Amelia was selected over other candidates because she displayed the "spirit and courageous skill" of her generation and their love of "new pioneering."

Amelia slept in the dorms among the students and encouraged them to think about what they wanted to do with their lives. Amelia discovered that 92 percent of the young women wanted careers.

Inspired by their ambition, Amelia felt she still had one more flying first she wanted to achieve before she gave it all up—to fly around the world. Pilot Wiley Post had performed a solo flight around the world two years earlier. If Amelia succeeded in this dangerous adventure, she would become the first woman to fly around the world. She couldn't resist the challenge.

Famous Fliers:
Wiley Post

Born: November 22, 1898

Wiley became fascinated by flying as a young man, after watching barnstormers perform daring stunts at air shows. He wanted to become one himself, and when a flier at his local airfield needed a new parachutist for his display, Wiley got the chance. Wiley's flying career almost came to an end when a drilling accident at the oil field where he worked caused a serious eye injury. He had to have his eye removed, but Wiley didn't let that stand in his way. On July 22, 1933, Wiley became the first person to fly around the world solo. He did it in 7 days, 18 hours, and 49 minutes.

Flier fact: While flying, Wiley wore a specially designed pressure suit to help him breathe at high altitudes, where oxygen levels are low.

CHAPTER 7

ONE MORE GOOD FLIGHT

To complete the "shining adventure" of flying nearly 29,000 miles around the world, Amelia would need a new plane. The one she chose was a Lockheed Electra 10E, equipped with all the latest dials and gadgets, including an early form of autopilot, which allowed aircraft to maintain their speed and trajectory without pilots having to be at the controls. To buy this plane, Amelia got help from her friends at Purdue, who bought the aircraft for the university as a kind of "laboratory" in the sky to encourage students to take up aviation. It arrived on Amelia's thirty-ninth birthday.

Great Planes:
Lockheed Electra 10E

Seats: 12

Wingspan: 55 ft. (16.8 m)

Manufacturer: Lockheed

Engine: Two air-cooled,
supercharged, nine-
cylinder radial engines

Horsepower: 600 hp

Speed: 177 mph (285 kmh)

Max height: 19,400 ft. (5,913 m)

Weight: 6,454 lb. (2,927 kg)

Date of manufacture: 1934

⋝ NO EXPENSE SPARED ⋜

A new plane was not the only preparation to be made.
For such a long trip, Amelia decided to hire a navigator
to help keep her on course. She chose Captain Harry
Manning for the task. He had been the captain of the
SS *President Roosevelt,* the ship that brought Amelia
and the crew of *Friendship* back from England in 1928.
Harry was a skilled radio operator and had many years'
experience crossing the globe by sea. After a number
of test flights, Amelia and George decided a second
navigator was needed for the trip, one more familiar
with navigating by air. They chose Fred Noonan, an
accomplished aviator and former navigator for Pan
American Airways.

Amelia also needed permission to land in all the
countries along her route. Luckily, her powerful
friends, including the Roosevelts, persuaded other
governments to allow her to land. Amelia and George
invested almost everything they had to pay for the trip,
hoping to make the money back with lecture tours,
book sales, and merchandise once Amelia returned.

On February 11, 1937, Amelia revealed her plans at
a press conference at the Barclay Hotel in New York.

⋛ READY TO GO ⋚

By March 17, 1937, Amelia was prepared. She, Harry
Manning, and Fred Noonan took off from Oakland,
California. Loaded with the 947 gallons (3,585 l) of
fuel they needed for the long flight, they set off for
Honolulu, Hawaii, on the first leg of their trip.

In Honolulu, Amelia and her crew planned to rest
and refuel before taking off, but bad weather meant
their takeoff was delayed for twenty-four hours. When
they did get clearance for takeoff, things did not go
smoothly. As Amelia sped down the runway, the plane
began to swerve. She adjusted the engines to try to
regain control, but it didn't work.

The plane, loaded with highly flammable jet fuel,
spun on the runway and tipped to the right side,
damaging the landing gear, right wing, and right
engine. A rogue spark could have turned the aircraft
into a fireball. To help prevent this, Amelia switched
off the ignition. Amelia was shaken, but she, Fred, and
Harry were unhurt.

The Electra had not been so lucky. Amelia's plane
needed to be shipped back to California, where it would
take three months and twenty-five thousand dollars

to repair the damage. They would have to go home. Amelia's attempt to fly around the world was over before it had even really begun.

But Amelia didn't give up. On her return to California, she immediately started to make plans for another attempt. Weather conditions had changed, and after consulting with meteorologists and flying experts, Amelia and Fred decided they would reverse their route. They would also be flying without Harry, who was unable to extend his leave from his job.

What to Pack?

As with all of Amelia's "long hops," or long flights, everything that wasn't essential was stripped from the aircraft to make the plane as light as possible, as well as to allow room for the extra fuel. Usually, Amelia didn't pack a change of clothes, but this trip would be so long that she took a small suitcase with five shirts, two pairs of trousers, a change of shoes, a rain jacket, and toiletries.

SECOND TIME LUCKY

On the morning of June 1, 1937, Amelia and Fred were ready to make their second attempt. Amelia smiled at the gathered reporters and cameras before giving George a goodbye kiss and climbing into the cockpit. They took off at 5:56 a.m. from Miami Municipal Airport, Florida. The plane rose into the sky without any problems. They were on their way.

Fred sat at the back of the plane at his navigation table, consulting charts to help guide them on their journey. The plane was so packed with fuel tanks that it was hard to reach the cockpit, and the noise from the Electra's engines made talking difficult, so the pair communicated with small notes that they attached to the line of a fishing rod, using the reel to pass them back and forth.

One of their first stops was San Juan, Puerto Rico, where they spent the night in the home of Puerto Rican aviator Clara Livingston. The next morning they took off for Caripito, Venezuela, to refuel.

They rested and refueled at each stop. Amelia was very disciplined, getting up hours before they were scheduled to take off to make preflight checks on the plane and their equipment. Much of the flying during this leg of the trip was over dense jungle, and Amelia feared crash-landing among the never-ending trees, so far away from rescue.

From Brazil, Amelia flew thirteen hours and twelve minutes across the Atlantic Ocean to reach Saint-Louis, Senegal, in Africa. What had once been a major achievement—crossing the Atlantic by air—now formed only a small part of her journey around the world.

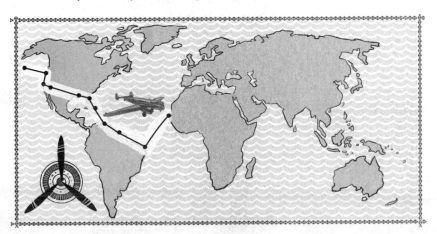

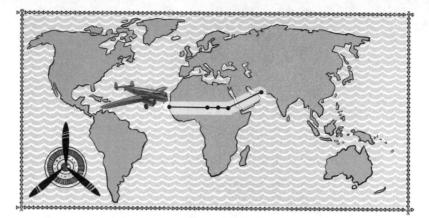

From Assab, Eritrea, Amelia flew for thirteen hours and ten minutes into the record books yet again when she made the first nonstop flight across the Red Sea to Karachi in what is now Pakistan (then India). With such a grueling schedule, Amelia and Fred weren't able to see much of the countries they stopped in, but after the long flight, they took a short break and found the time to ride camels.

From Karachi, they flew to Calcutta, India, using the network of railways crisscrossing the country to help them navigate. At one point, they were surrounded by black eagles that flew alarmingly close to the plane.

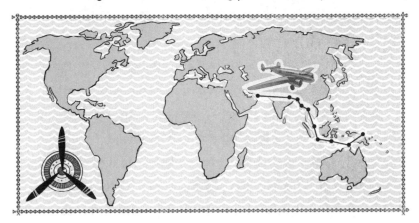

⋛ TRAVEL SICK ⋚

The long hours of flying were taking their toll on the Electra and on Amelia and Fred. After a long delay in Burma due to a monsoon, suffering from a stomach bug in Bandung, and Fred's airsickness from the smell of the fumes, both of them were ready to go home. On the island of Lae, Amelia wrote of the long stretch of ocean left to fly over:

I shall be glad when we have the hazards of its navigation behind us.

But the end was in sight. They had flown twenty-two thousand miles, with only seven thousand still to go. Amelia and Fred knew the remaining stretch would be some of the most hazardous flying yet—miles upon miles over open ocean. Fred and Amelia spent their days on Lae getting the plane ready for the trip.

They stripped the Electra of everything they didn't need for the hop, boxing up notebooks, souvenirs, and excess clothes to be shipped home. They wanted the plane as light as possible for the long journey that lay ahead of them—an eighteen-hour flight to Howland Island in the Pacific Ocean. Howland Island is tiny, measuring just two miles long and a half mile wide, and standing only twenty feet (six meters) above the ocean. Amelia and Fred spent extra time studying their maps and planning their route—they knew the smallest miscalculation could lead to disaster. They took off from the Lae airfield, built especially for Amelia's attempt, at midnight on July 2.

⋛ RADIO PROBLEMS ⋚

Seven hours and twenty minutes into the flight, Amelia reported her position as not being far from the Nukumanu Islands in the southwestern Pacific Ocean.

The message was picked up by a radio operator for New Guinea Airways. This was the only time during this leg of the trip that her radio worked as it should. After this, Amelia was only able to transmit messages and wasn't able to receive them. Something was seriously wrong.

Anchored off the coast of Howland Island, the crew of the coast guard ship *Itasca* waited with their radio to help guide Amelia and Fred to a safe landing. Amelia thought she was close, radioing to the *Itasca:*

"We must be on you but cannot see you but gas is running low. Been unable to reach you by radio. We are flying at altitude one thousand feet. Please take a bearing on us and answer on 3105 with voice."

The signal was so strong on her transmission that a member of the *Itasca* crew ran out on deck to listen for the Electra's engines, thinking it must be near. But there was no sign of Amelia. The *Itasca* radioed again and again, but it was clear Amelia wasn't receiving their transmissions. In her final transmission, at 8:43 a.m. local time, Amelia gave her position and said, "We are running north and south." This meant that they were flying from north to south searching for the *Itasca* and Howland Island.

Amelia, Fred, and the Lockheed Electra never landed on Howland Island. The commander of the *Itasca* waited just over an hour for more transmissions before beginning the search for the lost plane.

⋛ THE SEARCH BEGINS ⋛

In New York, George waited anxiously for news. He hoped the reports that the *Itasca* had lost contact with Amelia were false, but even if they were true, he knew what a skilled flier Amelia was and was sure she'd be all right.

"She has more courage than anyone I know. I am worried, of course, but I have confidence in her ability to handle any situation."
—George Putnam

But courage and confidence, which had carried Amelia through so many times before, were not enough this time. Preliminary searches by the *Itasca* found no sign of Amelia and her plane.

The Electra had been low on fuel, which meant if she had landed at sea, the plane may have floated, but Amelia's last transmissions didn't give much information as to where she might have crashed. After the *Itasca* failed to locate her, a navy seaplane was brought in to look from the air.

British ships in the area also joined the search, and more US Navy ships combed the sea, sending men to search nearby islands. There were reports of flares being spotted and radio transmissions received, but they ultimately led to nothing. As the hours and days passed, the chances of finding Amelia and Fred became very low.

The Search

The search for Amelia and Fred was the biggest and most expensive search ever conducted by the US Navy at the time. It cost almost $5 million. Over 4,000 military personnel, 60 aircraft, and 10 ships were involved in the search, which covered 250,000 square miles (647,497 sq. km)—an area about the size of France.

Sixteen days after their last transmission, Amelia and Fred were declared lost at sea, and the official search was called off. George refused to give up, though, even despite his money running low. To help finance the search, George published the book Amelia had been writing about the trip from notes she sent back from Lae. He titled the book *Last Flight*. But even with the extra funds from the book, no sign of the Electra, Amelia, or Fred was found.

⋛ SAYING GOODBYE ⋚

People held services for Amelia around the country, including one in New York on November 21, 1937. Two hundred men and women gathered at Floyd Bennett Field to pay tribute to Amelia.

Planes flew in formation overhead as friends praised Amelia's "deathless spirit," and messages were read from Eleanor Roosevelt and Lou Gordon.

"Amelia did not lose, because her last flight was endless. Like in a relay race of progress, she has merely placed the torch in the hands of others to carry on to the next goal and from there on and on forever." —Jacqueline Cochran, Amelia's friend and a women's flight speed record holder

On January 5, 1939, a year and a half after she disappeared, Amelia was legally declared dead. George remarried in May 1939 but continued his efforts to find Amelia and stayed in contact with her family, providing them with support from her estate until his death in 1960.

Remembering Amelia

Since Amelia's disappearance, many memorials have been dedicated to her and her achievements.

Amelia Earhart Lighthouse

In 1937, the US government built a lighthouse on Howland Island in preparation for Amelia's attempt to fly around the world. After her disappearance, the lighthouse was named in her honor.

Amelia Earhart Birthplace Museum

Amelia's grandparents' house in Atchison, Kansas—her home until she was twelve years old—was turned into a museum by the Ninety-Nines. In September each year, members of the Ninety-Nines meet there, after flying into the local airport, named Amelia Earhart Memorial Airport.

Amelia Earhart Peak

In 1967, a mountain in Yosemite National Park was named Amelia Earhart Peak in honor of Amelia, who had enjoyed visiting the park.

Amelia Earhart Memorial

In 2007, 75 years after her solo flight across the Atlantic, a statue of Amelia Earhart was built in Harbour Grace, Canada, in memory of her special connection to the town.

WHAT HAPPENED TO AMELIA?

In the years since Amelia's death, there have been many theories as to what happened to her.

Theory one: captured

Amelia crashed in the ocean, and she and Fred were picked up by the Japanese navy and held prisoner. Japan was hostile toward the United States at this time, believing that America was trying to stop overseas expansion of the Japanese empire.

Theory two: out of the spotlight

Amelia had grown tired of her dangerous life and all the publicity and so faked her own death. She returned secretly to the United States to live out her days free from the press as a homemaker in New Jersey.

Theory three: marooned

Amelia and Fred crash-landed somewhere near Nikumaroro Island, 350 nautical miles (about 650 km) from Howland Island. In 1940, thirteen bones were discovered on the island, which experts say may have belonged to Amelia. Other evidence found on the otherwise-uninhabited island included a pot that may have contained freckle cream, and fragments of an airplane. Unfortunately, the bone fragments were lost before DNA testing could be done to confirm whether they belonged to Amelia.

Theory four: secret agent

Amelia had been on a secret US government spy mission and could turn up at any time during the years following her death.

Even now, eighty years after her last fateful flight, new theories continue to emerge. Teams still search for the remains of Amelia's aircraft, scouring the depths of the Pacific Ocean using the most up-to-date equipment.

CONCLUSION

LOOKING FOR A LEGEND

The fact that people are still looking for answers so many years after Amelia's disappearance shows what an impact she had. From the brave little girl who liked nothing better than to slam her sled down snowy hills and explore caves along the Missouri River, Amelia grew up to take on the whole world. She worked hard to transform herself into a record-breaking aviator and icon. At the time of her disappearance, Amelia had broken countless flying records, written bestselling books, received awards from world leaders, and become a regular visitor to the White House.

People are fascinated by Amelia, not just because of her records and achievements, but because of what she represented.

As a young girl, Amelia looked for examples of women who were breaking barriers. She clipped articles from newspapers and magazines. These explorers, lawyers, and doctors showed Amelia that a life filled with adventures was possible and inspired her to live one of her own. Amelia wanted her achievements to motivate the women who came after her.

> I want to do it because I want to do it. Women must do things as men have tried. When they fail, their failure must be but a challenge to others.

Many have taken up Amelia's challenge and credit her for inspiring them to achieve their own dreams. These people include former US secretary of state and 2016 presidential candidate Hillary Clinton.

"After learning that Amelia Earhart kept a scrapbook with newspaper articles about successful women in male-dominated jobs, I started a scrapbook of my own."
—Hillary Clinton

Associate Justice of the US Supreme Court Ruth Bader Ginsburg was also influenced by Amelia, claiming that as a child her heroes were fictional detective Nancy Drew and "Amelia Earhart, who was doing something that women just didn't do in her day."

⋛ CONTRIBUTION TO FLYING ⋛

Amelia was not the first woman to fly a plane. Even by her own admission, she wasn't the most talented female pilot of the era. However, her good humor and down-to-earth attitude made her popular among her peers. As president of the Ninety-Nines, Amelia encouraged countless women to take to the skies.

Jacqueline Cochran

During World War II, Jacqueline helped form the Women's Airforce Service Pilots (WASP) and was the first woman to fly a bomber across the Atlantic. After the war, Jacqueline became the first woman to break the sound barrier. During her lifetime, Jacqueline broke more records in aviation than any other flier, male or female.

Willa Brown

In 1938, many airfields in America had racist rules that prevented African Americans from flying. In Chicago, Willa found a place where she could learn, becoming the first African American woman to earn her private pilot's license in the United States, and later the first African American woman to earn a commercial pilot's license. In 1946, Willa turned to politics, campaigning for civil rights and becoming the first African American woman to run for the US Congress.

Emily Howell Warner

In 1976, Emily Howell Warner became the first woman to command an American passenger flight. After years of working as a flying instructor and applying to airlines, Emily was employed by Frontier Airlines as a first officer and was eventually made a captain.

Jeannie M. Leavitt

On February 10, 1994, Jeannie became the first woman to qualify as a combat pilot in the US Air Force. Jeannie challenged rules that stopped women from serving in combat situations and became a brigadier responsible for 34 air force squadrons across America.

Sally Ride

Sally was the first American woman to travel into space, in 1983. She was also the youngest person ever in space.
After leaving NASA, Sally spent her career helping women and girls achieve their dreams of studying science and mathematics.

⋛ A SMALL WORLD ⋛

People all over America were inspired to visit some of
the exciting places Amelia had written about. As planes
became safer and airfares cheaper, more passengers
climbed aboard and explored places their parents would
have only known about from world's fairs. In 1937, the
world sat on the edge of their seats listening to the radio
for reports on one woman's flight around the world. Today,
there can be more than sixteen thousand aircraft in the
air at any time. In 2018, it was estimated that more than
three billion people traveled by plane.

≍ AMELIA'S STORY ≍

Amelia's adventurous life and mysterious disappearance have also inspired hundreds of books, dozens of movies, and a few songs. There was even a dance called the Earhart Hop.

Amelia wrote three books of her own about her life: *20 Hrs., 40 Min: Our Flight in the* Friendship (1928); *The Fun of It* (1932); and *Last Flight* (1937), compiled by George from her notes and published after her disappearance. Following her death, many more books were written about her life, including *Courage Is the Price* (1963), by her sister, Muriel.

In 1943, *Flight for Freedom,* a film inspired by Amelia, was released in movie theaters. The film starred Rosalind Russell as female aviator Tonie Carter, who disappears during her attempt to fly around the world. In 1976, a television movie called *Amelia Earhart* depicted Amelia's career from the age of twenty-three until her disappearance in 1937. Actress Diane Keaton won a Golden Globe for her portrayal of Amelia in the 1994 movie *Amelia Earhart: The Final Flight.*

The most recent biopic about her life, *Amelia,* was released in 2009. The movie starred Hilary Swank in the title role and Richard Gere as George. The movie was based on a biography called *The Sound of Wings* by Mary S. Lovell.

There have also been many documentaries exploring the theories surrounding Amelia's disappearance and searching for the wreckage of her lost Electra. In 2019, National Geographic Channel premiered a film documenting the search for Amelia's lost plane, titled *Expedition Amelia.* The famous explorer and discoverer of the wreck of the RMS *Titanic,* Robert Ballard, led the multimillion-dollar search using the most up-to-date equipment.

FLYING INTO THE FUTURE

To this day, Amelia's story challenges people all over the world to lead lives filled with adventure, and to strive to achieve their goals. Not everyone will be given the opportunities to break records or fly their own plane like Amelia was, but her achievements show what incredible things can happen when people dare to dream and say yes to adventures. Amelia may have been lost, but her courage, confidence, and spirit will live on forever.

Everyone has his own Atlantics to fly. Whatever you want very much to do, against the opposition of tradition, neighborhood opinion, and so-called "common sense"—that is an Atlantic.

Timeline

July 24
Amelia Mary Earhart is born in Atchison, Kansas.

July 28
World War I begins in Europe.

1897   1903   1914

December 17
Orville and Wilbur Wright make the first flight in a powered airplane in Kitty Hawk, North Carolina.

Amelia takes her first flying lesson with Neta Snook at Rogers Field, California.
Amelia buys her first plane, a Kinner Airster, which she names *The Canary*.

1920   1921

Amelia takes her first plane ride with Frank Monroe Hawks and decides she wants to learn to fly.

1917

December
Amelia becomes a nurse's assistant at Spadina Military Hospital in Toronto, Canada.

1918

November 11
World War I ends.

April
Amelia receives a call from Captain H. Railey asking if she would like to become the first woman to fly across the Atlantic.

Amelia's parents get divorced.

1924   1927   1928

May 21
Charles Lindbergh becomes the first man to fly across the Atlantic.

June 18
Amelia becomes the first woman to cross the Atlantic by air, as a passenger on board *Friendship*.

1928   1929   1931

November 2
Amelia and other female pilots form the Ninety-Nines.

February 7
Amelia marries George Putnam.

January 12
Amelia becomes the first person to fly solo across the Pacific Ocean from Honolulu, Hawaii, to Oakland, California.

March 20
Amelia crashes her plane on Ford Island, Hawaii, while taking off for the second leg of her round-the-world flight.

1935   1937

May 21
Amelia becomes the first woman and second person ever to fly across the Atlantic solo.

Amelia visits the White House as a guest of President Franklin Roosevelt.

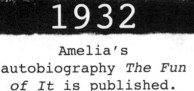

1932

1933

Amelia's autobiography *The Fun of It* is published.

July 2
Amelia and Fred fail to arrive at Howland Island in the Pacific Ocean. They are declared lost at sea sixteen days later.

January 5
Amelia Earhart is declared dead.

1939

June 1
Amelia and navigator Fred Noonan take off from Miami, Florida, for her second attempt to fly around the world.

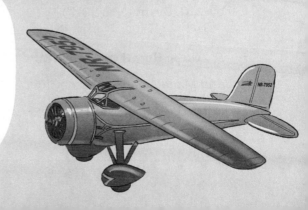

Further Reading

→ *Amelia Earhart* by Libby Romero
   (DK Life Stories, 2020)

→ *Amelia Lost: The Life and Disappearance of Amelia Earhart* by Candace Fleming (Yearling, 2019)

→ *Flight: The Complete History of Aviation* by R. G. Grant (DK, 2017)

→ *Fly Girls: How Five Daring Women Defied All Odds and Made Aviation History* by Keith O'Brien (HMH Books for Young Readers, 2019)

Websites

→ ameliaearhart.com
The official licensing website of Amelia Earhart, including photographs of Amelia, her most famous quotes, and her life story.

→ ninety-nines.org
Find out more about women in aviation history at the website of the international organization of licensed women pilots, cofounded by Amelia Earhart and her contemporaries.

→ pioneersofflight.si.edu/people
A website from the Smithsonian National Air and Space Museum, including rare photographs and more information about the world's most famous fliers.

Glossary

alcoholism: A medical disorder that can cause people to drink alcohol to a point where it has a negative impact on their lives and the lives of those around them.

altimeter: An instrument used for measuring an aircraft's height above sea level.

altitude: The height of an object above sea level.

autopilot: A device able to steer an aircraft in place of a person.

aviation: The practice of building and flying aircraft.

aviatrix: A female pilot.

barnstormer: A person who performs daring flight demonstrations at air shows.

Glossary

bluff: A high, steep area of land usually situated near a body of water.

commonwealth: A group of nations with economic connections to one another.

corset: A stiff undergarment worn by a woman that, when fastened tightly, makes her waist appear smaller.

dispensary: A place where medicine is measured out for patients.

exposition: A show or exhibition open to the public.

finishing school: A place where wealthy young women were sent by their families to prepare them for their role in society.

Glossary

hop: A slang term for a short flight.

meteorologist: A scientist who studies and predicts the weather.

pontoon: Air-filled cylinders attached to an aircraft in place of wheels to allow the aircraft to take off and land on water.

seaplane: An aircraft able to take off and land on water.

stock market: The place where traders buy and sell shares of companies.

suffrage: The right to vote in an election.

transatlantic: Crossing the Atlantic Ocean.

transmission: A message or broadcast that is sent by radio.

Glossary

turbulent: Moving in a violent and unpredictable way.

wing walk: An aerial stunt involving walking out onto the wings of an aircraft while in flight.

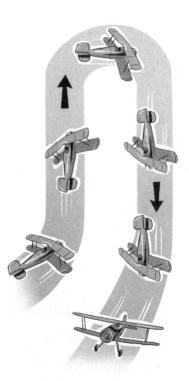

Index

Index

Index

Index

FOLLOW THE TRAIL!

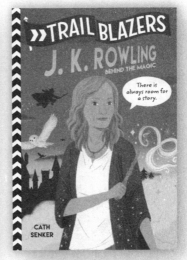

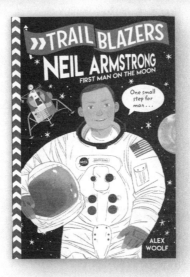

TURN THE PAGE FOR A SNEAK PEEK AT THESE TRAILBLAZERS BIOGRAPHIES!

Trailblazers: Lin-Manuel Miranda excerpt text copyright © 2021
by Kurtis Scaletta.
Illustrations copyright © 2021 by David Shephard.
Cover art copyright © 2021 by Luisa Uribe.
Published in the United States by Random House Children's Books,
a division of Penguin Random House LLC, New York.

≋ A HOUSE FULL OF MUSIC ≋

The Miranda house was always full of music, especially soundtracks to films and plays. Family favorites included *Camelot*, *Man of La Mancha*, and *The Unsinkable Molly Brown*. Growing up in a house where show tunes were always on the record player, Lin-Manuel "never had a chance to be anything but a musical theater guy," he has said.

The family also loved Latin music—the music of their roots—and Luis and Luz taught their children how to dance salsa.

Lin-Manuel's favorite musical as a child was a movie—*The Little Mermaid*. He particularly liked Sebastian the crab and his song "Under the Sea." When the song was nominated for an Oscar for Best Original Song in a movie in 1989, Lin-Manuel took interest in the awards show for the first time. As he watched with his family, he promised his mother if *he* ever went to the Oscars, she would be his date on the red carpet.

His feelings about music ran deep. He would burst into tears when listening to certain songs, such as Simon & Garfunkel's "Bridge over Troubled Water" or Stevie Wonder's "I Just Called to Say I Love You." Little Lin-Manuel would try to sing along but would break down with emotion before he reached the chorus. He loved movies with lots of songs but couldn't make it through *Mary Poppins*, either. He'd be too upset by the sadness of "Feed the Birds," a song about a homeless woman, to keep watching.

"In the character of Hamilton—
a striving immigrant who escaped
poverty, made his way to the New
World, climbed to the top by sheer
force of will and pluck and
determination—Lin-Manuel saw
something of his own family, and
every immigrant family."
—Barack Obama

Michelle simply described it as "the best piece of art in any form I have ever seen."

That day, the cast performed the show without the usual staging and costumes, but still electrified the room. The highlight of the event, though, was a freestyle rap by Lin-Manuel and the president in the Rose Garden. Lin-Manuel was able to draw from his Freestyle Love Supreme experience to make up rhymes on the spot as Barack held up cards with terms like "Oval Office," "Congress," and "Constitution," which Lin-Manuel deftly turned into a rhyme. The performance was streamed live on the White House website.

I can't believe I'm there; it's so much more intimidating than if it was square.
OVAL OFFICE

Trailblazers: J. K. Rowling excerpt text copyright © 2020
by Cath Senker.
Illustrations copyright © 2020 by Tom Heard.
Cover art copyright © 2020 by Luisa Uribe.
Published in the United States by Random House Children's Books,
a division of Penguin Random House LLC, New York.

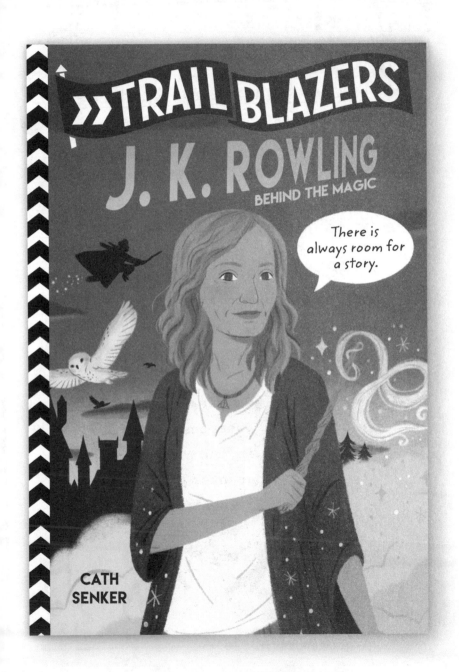

The Swinging Sixties

The late 1960s were a time of considerable cultural change in the United Kingdom, the United States, and other countries. Bands such as the Beatles and the Rolling Stones were revolutionizing the music industry, and young people wore daring new fashions: brightly colored clothes, tiny miniskirts, and widely flared, or bell-bottom, jeans. Some people were inspired to become involved in social movements—for example, campaigning against nuclear weapons or against the US involvement in the Vietnam War. Even Joanne's parents, in their small village, were influenced by the new culture. They loved dancing to Beatles records in their living room.

AN IMAGINATIVE GIRL

Peter and Anne enjoyed reading, and their home was full of books. They always read to the girls at bedtime. Joanne especially loved fantasy and classic books. When she was four, she caught the measles and was stuck in bed for days. Her dad read Kenneth Grahame's *The Wind in the Willows* to her, with tales of the animal characters Rat, Mole, Toad, and Badger, who live in the English countryside and go on adventures.

Trailblazers: Neil Armstrong excerpt text copyright © 2019
by Alex Woolf.
Illustrations copyright © 2019 by Artful Doodlers.
Cover art copyright © 2019 by Luisa Uribe and George Ermos.
Published in the United States by Random House Children's Books,
a division of Penguin Random House LLC, New York.

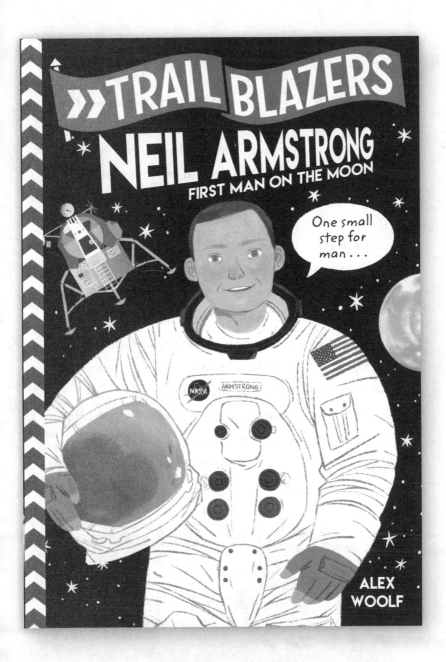

⋝ FLYING LESSONS ⋜

Airplanes remained Neil's first love. His dream was to become both a pilot and an aeronautical engineer— someone who designs and builds planes. About three or four miles outside Wapakoneta was Port Koneta Airport. Neil cycled or hitchhiked there as often as he could to watch the planes land and take off, and talk to the pilots.

When he was fifteen, Neil began saving up for flying lessons. He got a job at Rhine and Brading's Pharmacy, where he earned forty cents an hour. A one-hour flying lesson cost nine dollars, so he had to work twenty-two and a half hours to pay for one lesson! Neil supplemented his earnings at the pharmacy by offering to wash down the airplanes at Port Koneta. He even helped the airport mechanics with some routine maintenance work, servicing the planes' cylinders, pistons, and valves.

Eventually, Neil had saved up enough money to pay for some lessons. A veteran army pilot named Aubrey Knudegard taught him. They flew in a light, high-wing monoplane called an Aeronca Champion.

Aircraft Fact File

Name:	Aeronca Champion
Nickname:	"Champ"
Length:	21.5 ft. (6.6 m)
Wingspan:	35.2 ft. (10.7 m)
Engine:	65 horsepower
Top speed:	100 mph (161 kmh)
First flight:	April 29, 1944